Walks *in the* Dark

MICHAEL CAMPISI

ISBN 978-1-64191-959-3 (paperback)
ISBN 978-1-64191-960-9 (digital)

Christian Faith Publishing, Inc.
832 Park Avenue
Meadville, PA 16335
www.christianfaithpublishing.com

Printed in the United States of America

Dedicated to my wife and mother of our children,
Tracey Lynn Campisi,
and to the memory of our son,
Maverick Albert Campisi
9/29/99–6/17/16
Forever Sixteen.
Equals Awesome.

ACKNOWLEDGMENTS

I wish to acknowledge a number of people that have provided support.

Tracey Campisi, for giving me counsel, guidance, and awareness education.

Logan Campisi, Maverick's big brother, for never turning his back on us or this situation. He is our rock.

Brenda Campisi – Maverick's big sister, for watching over Mom and being on-call to us.

David and Janine Campisi, by brother and sister-in-law, who came to our aid without hesitation and have always supported us.

Rod and Nancy Depperschmidt, my father-in-law and step–mother-in-law. They compassionately engaged us right away, asked questions, and always listened to our answers through our tears.

Dottie Depperschmidt, my mother-in-law, for everything, especially sending Maverick a birthday card his first birthday after. It meant more to us than you will ever know.

Ben Smith, Maverick's best friend. If you need it, then you only need ask. We will do what we can.

Thad and Fiona Smith, Ben's father and stepmother. Thad, my co-worker, was my voice at work early on. They are always there to help and support us.

Zoe Flynn, Maverick's good friend and "wing girl." Thanks for the pictures and videos. If you need it, then you only need ask. We will do what we can.

Sean and Jessie Flynn, Zoe's father and stepmother. Big Maverick fans. Thanks for listening to us and supporting our events.

Tirso Rosario, co-worker and one of my first phone calls as his son, Nick, knew Maverick. He became my staunch protector at work.

Kristi and Jerry DeFalco, my cousin and her husband, who sent us food the first week and frequently checked on us.

Brad and Iva Hollenberg, best friend from work and his wife, who came to us four days after Maverick died. Thanks for the counsel and direction. Sorry for your loss.

Nicholas Campisi, thanks for hanging with us and Logan during our toughest times.

Dr. Mitch Stevison, my boss, who provided a calm voice on the other end of the phone when I really needed it, who frequently checks on me and reads my poems. He was one of the first that told me to write this book.

Sean Riley, my younger brother from work, thanks for coming to our aid the first week.

Our neighbors. Many brought us food the first week.

Leadership, peers, staff, and people at my company who came to Maverick's memorial, check on me, and take it upon themselves to protect my privacy.

Andrew Braunreiter, good friend of Maverick, you are doing well. Stay the course.

Mia Schneider, thanks for some of the best pictures of Maverick. The sunset one is my favorite.

Hannah Pastor, big Maverick fan with a huge heart. She is like a daughter to Tracey.

Tori Cole, you tried really hard to find out what was wrong with Maverick in the last week. We will always remember that and how supportive you are of us.

Maverick's many other friends. They gave us many pictures, stories, videos, and kind words.

Ms. Natalie Brunett, principal, and the staff of Ironwood Ridge High School. They have put up with our many requests for memorial items and awareness events.

My crowd. Grieving parents that engage with me and provide counsel, insight, and compassion.

Society for the prevention of teen suicide who gave me great insight and support.

INTRODUCTION

MY NAME IS MIKE. I am an American, Christian, husband to Tracey, and father to three children: Brenda, Logan, and Maverick. Tracey and I married in 1991. She is ten years my junior. We had our first child, Brenda, in 1992. Logan was born in 1995. Maverick was born in 1999. All our children were born in Arizona.

I have lived in and out of Arizona thirty-one of my fifty-seven years. I was born in Phoenix. I went to high school in Tucson and graduated from Arizona State University in Tempe. In between different stops in Arizona, I lived overseas and multiple states.

Twenty years ago, I started to get up very early to work out and get ready for my day. It was the only real "free time" I could find. My workouts include long walks. I am usually with one of our dogs, doing martial arts, saying my prayers, looking for shooting stars, and planning my work for the day. It is the time that I process events and issues and sort out what I will do next. In Tucson, there are regulations limiting light pollution in support of Kitt Peak Observatory. For the past five years, I have taken my "walks in the dark."

But this book isn't about me. It is about my family, and especially my son, Maverick.

Chapter 1

Our Maverick

MAVERICK ALBERT CAMPISI. BORN SEPTEMBER 29, 1999, a warm day in Tucson, Arizona. Date selected specifically by my wife. Maverick is our youngest of three and the second son. Seven years junior to his sister and four years junior to his brother. His name came from the movie *Top Gun* and his great-grandfather, Albert Schott (Grandpa Ab), a tall and righteous cowboy that I truly respected. We like that his entire name means "noble, independent, and bright."

Tracey had her labor induced at full term. It immediately sent both her and Maverick into distress. Quite the scare, but everything was quickly brought under control, and I took them both home the next day. The house settled into a standard cadence with our two older ones watching their new brother with curiosity and primal induced protection. We settled into ever important routine of standard rituals based on our agreed-to parental roles. Busy but not stressful. We had the "parenting thing" and our division of responsibilities pretty wired by our third offspring.

There were striking similarities and striking differences. Brenda with dark eyes, thick, wavy brown hair, and a growing artistic creativity. She looks like Tracey. Logan with green eyes, very curly light brown hair inherited from Tracey, physically coordinated, and tough. He looks and acts more like me. Maverick with his blue eyes, thick, dark hair that later turned blond, quick to smile, and strong attachment to Tracey. He looks a lot like Tracey. Early summer of 2000, when Maverick was crawling and just past a nasty bout of bronchitis, I took a job in the defense industry and moved the entire clan to Florida.

Florida

Florida was a good time for us as a family. We lived in a two-story house with a pool and a large backyard with a swing set and playhouse just outside St. Petersburg. The neighborhood was full of children in the age range of ours, and we lived near a large park with riding trails  and wildlife. Our two older ones were learning how to ride bikes, swim, fish, and build sandcastles on the beach. Maverick was working on walking. He was a charmer and was frequently the focus of attention at church or the store.

The children went through an "animal phase" during this period. Snakes, frogs, dog (Pepper), cats, ducks, and gerbils. Behavior that started in Arizona, Brenda was the real driver for all the acquisitions. But Logan caught on and started down the same path. Every weekend was a run to the pet store for some type of not-cheap food to feed the exotic animals. And yes, every once in a while, there was the frantic search for an escaped animal.

Tracey was growing an Avon business. We decided early on that we didn't want to have others raise our children. She hadn't worked since a week before we had Brenda. As if she didn't have enough with the three children and all the animals, she decided she wanted to make money and get out socially. It was the perfect job for her. She was very, very successful. Our house looked like a warehouse from time to time as orders came in. Everyone would pitch in to fill orders. The two older ones were in school, so it was Tracey and Maverick

running around town, taking orders and making deliveries.

My aunt and cousins lived in Orlando. Two of my cousins, Kim and Kristi, were characters at Disneyworld. They had family discounts, so we had extended stays at Disneyworld resorts at least three times a year. Brenda walking, Logan in the stroller, in my arms or on my shoulders, and Maverick usually in my backpack, we would stomp around the theme parks. Disney had a "stroller exchange" process where you walk up to any ride's exit and the parents would swap. Tracey and I would trade off Maverick and get on the ride with Brenda and Logan. We did this

until we got our fill and wanted to move on to another ride. We always made sure Maverick had something to keep him occupied, but the crowd and sounds seemed to be enough most times. All of us loved Cirque du Soleil in Downtown Disney, although we were concerned the profes-

sional acrobats were giving the boys far too many ideas. Maverick was just about the right height for all the rides when I took a job transfer to McKinney (North Dallas), Texas. We moved in late 2004.

Texas

Texas was a time of great growth for all of us. Tracey and the kids started taking martial arts. Tracey moved onto intense yoga. Brenda graduated high school. Her artistic talent and intellectual skills now fully developed. Logan went through middle school and started high school. He lettered by playing the viola in school orchestra. Both the boys played baseball for years. Logan was a pitcher, and Maverick a big hitting short stop. Brenda and Logan both learned to drive. Brenda got a car. Brenda had boyfriends, and Logan had girlfriends. There was always something going on in our house or an event to attend. There were times we had to trade off children in a parking lot or at a fast food place so we could run them to the next event.

Maverick developed rapidly in Texas. Martial arts, baseball, starting school, learning to ride bikes, and

friends all influenced him. He started speaking his own mind and not shy to communicate his opinion. He and I had our first real disagreement when he came into the study to inform me he wasn't going to play baseball anymore. Tracey and I

14

enjoyed baseball as she was the dugout mom and I was the assistant coach. Maverick was a good player on a team of boys he had known for six years. I had a vision of hours of throwing the ball and batting practice flying out the window. But he had decided he wanted to play basketball, wanted me to pay for clinics, and put up a basket in the front drive. I was impressed with the thoughtful and comprehensive argument presented to me by my almost eleven-year-old. Of course, he used Tracey's mannerisms, which caught me off guard. I also made a mental note that he ran right over me much like Tracey does when she has her mind set.

This was also a period of extensive travel for us as a family. We decided we needed to have our children experience different places. We took them to Washington, DC, so they could see that the location was

more than pictures in a history book. We went through several of the Smithsonians, visited many of the monuments, and watched the changing of the guard at the tomb of the unknown soldier at Arlington.

We took them on two cruises. The first was combined with my cousin's (Kristi) wedding in Florida. We decided to take them to Jamaica and Grand Cayman. The boys were pretty

excited about the 24-7 pizza and ice cream on the ship. Several years later, we took the clan on a cruise to Alaska. We visited fisheries, looked for bears, watched the eagles, panned for gold, visited the Yukon, and visited a glacier. We had a day in Seattle when we got back, so we had to go to the space needle. Tracey and I always felt it was important for us to invest in good memories for our children.

I took another job while in Texas, which required extensive travel. I always asked everyone what they wanted from wherever I would be that week. Tracey usually wanted a refrigerator magnet and Maverick always wanted a "dream catcher." He would always have a big smile when I presented him the latest dream catcher find. They ultimately covered the walls in his room and was a source of pride for him. Maverick was given the choice, like all the kids did, of a pet for his tenth birthday. He chose a dog and Tracey chose a Yorkshire terrier that we named "Ziggy." Ziggy became very attached to Tracey and Tracey to him. Ziggy and the dream catchers are important later in this story.

Since Brenda was born, we traveled to Colorado at least each summer for a week to visit Tracey's parents and grandmother. My mother-in-law and grandmother-in-law lived on two large adjoining horse properties in Loveland, north of Denver. Having to be busy, I would always ask for lists of things that needed to get done. It was a good chance to do needed chores and teach my children the value of work. We cleaned orchards, dug irrigation ditches, spread rock, trimmed trees, cleaned out gutters, painted, and anything else we could find that needed doing. A key part of our trips was our annual visit to Estes

Park. We would always take a family old time portrait and usually travel into the Rocky Mountain National Park to hike by the Big Thompson. As they got older, the boys became bolder on our hikes. Logan would usually start it and Maverick would do everything in his power to keep up. We would end our days playing cards or board games at the dinner table. Lots of laughter and competition. These are special times in my memory.

I took a transfer to a job in Tucson, Arizona, in the summer of 2012.

Back in Arizona

The move to Arizona was very difficult for us. We had lived in Texas for almost eight years. With all of life's changes, we had accumulated a lot of things. Homes were not selling well in Texas but were selling very well in Arizona. We quickly found we would have to pay double for a house two-thirds the size. Brenda was in community college and had a boyfriend, but realized she couldn't yet support herself. So she was moving with us. Logan just finished his sophomore year of high school and was doing very well in orchestra. Maverick just finished sixth grade and was very much into basketball. So Tracey and I were presented with a move into an

environment that had few four-bedroom homes, finding a home that had the right schools with the right offerings, sizing down from four thousand square feet to around three thousand square feet, a big hit to our budget, moving the animals, and we didn't know if we could even sell the Texas home.

Tracey and I took two relocation trips to Tucson. We looked at over forty homes, including foreclosures, and couldn't make everything match up. We ended up moving the clan into a three-bedroom temporary housing apartment in August of 2012. Arizona schools were about to start, so the pressure was on. Taking my walks in the dark, I was begging for help. It was a warm Saturday morning when Maverick started telling me that the house *had* to have a pool. He had thought about it, so I knew I would get run over. "It will help all of us to stay cool. Oh, and it has to be heated for winter use." That very Saturday, my Texas realtor called me with a cash offer on our Texas home. That afternoon, our Arizona realtor took us to a house we hadn't seen before. Custom-made and upgraded four-bedroom/four-bath on four acres of desert landscape, long entry drive with attached two-car garage and RV garage with three very large storage rooms, two fenced backyards, and fenced entryway. It is on a one-mile dead end road with similar homes. Oh yeah, it has a heated pool and had schools we wanted. Everything was done that weekend. Prayers answered.

The next two years were full of change and adjustment. Brenda moved into her own place. She had a job and was going to community college. I found a new definition of "nanosecond." It was the time between Brenda carrying the last box out of the house and Maverick moving into her bedroom. She had the pick of rooms as the oldest and Maverick always had his eye on it since it was bigger and had an adjoining bathroom. She started moving out, and he started pestering her to "get it done." He completely moved in  that day. Logan jumped back into martial arts, played music, and worked at an elderly home as part of a high school nurse training program. He graduated high school in 2014. He decided to stay home, go to community college, and got a job at Walmart.

Maverick's life and personality expanded during middle school. He played basketball but was starting to turn toward volleyball. He quickly developed a set of friends, "his crowd," "his peeps," "his fam." His social skills grew quickly along with his social confidence. All of us noticed and frequently commented about his skills. He became humorous and a source of enter-  tainment. This was when the "almost every weekend" sleepovers started. He had a lot of friends, but there were a couple that were always around: Ben and Andrew. He started developing his own style. Certain clothes, hats, and shoes. Nothing from Walmart or Target. He started to want "Hollister" and "Abercrombie." He wanted to shop at places like "Tilly's." He started wearing his hats backward at times and his hairstyle was changing. Girls were becom- ing interesting to him. He always liked the girls, and they always liked him back. Girl interest combined with his social skills put Tracey and me on con- stant "parent alert." Maverick graduated eighth grade the same week Logan graduated high school.

During his eighth grade year, I bought a motorcycle. Rode it  back and forth to work most days. A twen- ty-seven-mile ride one way. Would also ride Maverick around to or from different social events. On the weekends, Tracey and I took to riding to one of the local national or state parks to hike a trail or two. We eventually came to like Catalina State Park, north of Tucson, and would walk there once or twice a week. We found the walks to be a perfect augmentation of our weekly "date night" din- ners out. We would hike about an hour cov- ering all kinds of topics. Mostly centered on our children, our discussions focused on our perceptions, next steps, and "good cop/bad cop" guidance to each other. Establishing parental unity in the face of situations presented to us by our maturing boys. I found these walks a parallel to my daily walks in the dark.

Our walks quickly became part of our regular routine. Tracey and I have always tried to establish a fairly fixed cadence for the children. We ate dinner as a family six nights a week. On workdays, each family member would summarize their day for me so I could keep up. Saturday, we took the clan out to dinner. Had to be a place that served hamburgers (Chilli's was a favorite) as the boys were both hamburger fiends. We would then play card games or a board game before turning them loose. Sunday was "dinner and a movie" night. We took turns picking a family movie and watching while eating dinner. Logan was all about action and adventure. Maverick started that way and then leaned toward romantic comedies, very much like Tracey, the summer before his freshman year.

Our annual Colorado trip that year was a turning point for Maverick. He went through one of four significant "need a completely new wardrobe" growth spurts that summer. He surpassed Tracey and was now about Logan's height. His shoulders were spreading and he started gaining muscle. His physical coordination, a mainstay of Logan's world, improved dramatically. His infectious energy was rising rapidly. Maverick started using language as a tool. Sometimes inappropriate, but always with a bent of wit and humor, he would just pop something out of his mouth that would have us gasp and laugh at the same time. He flashed hand signs and walked with a boldness that kept everyone's attention. He held his own at the nightly dinner table games, yard work, and conversations. He was morphing into a man in front of us. His grandparents and step-uncle, Chris, noted the changes. Tracey and I decided to modify our interactions with him with a focus on preparing him for manhood and greater responsibility.

Freshman Year

Tracey and Maverick have always been close. They are very much alike in looks and mannerisms. She took him to freshman orientation and reported that we had no need to worry about the transition to high school. He was friends with everyone. Tracey and Maverick would watch movies together, go on "Starbucks runs," and go shopping for his clothes as her sense of style is far more honed than mine. She was his chauffeur to and from school, which allowed them to talk and share music. They were always interacting whether by text, phone, or face-to-face. On the spur of the moment, Tracey decided to take Maverick and his friend, Andrew, on a road trip to San Diego ("Cali" as Maverick would say) during fall break. Two nights turned into four. They came home in constant babble about the things they did and saw.

Maverick turned fifteen in September and had his second growth spurt around Christmas. We decided to take a road trip during winter break. Maverick insisted we go to "Cali." We got a hotel near Universal Studios in Los Angeles. A room for the boys and an adjoining room for us. We drove out. Spent four days

going to the theme park, Whisky a Go Go, Hollywood walk of fame, Santa Monica Pier, and Rodeo Drive. Our pictures of the trip

tell of the fun we had running around LA. He told me during that trip that he was going to move to Cali someday.

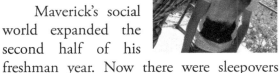

Maverick's social world expanded the second half of his freshman year. Now there were sleepovers with multiple boys. He was particularly close to Ben and Andrew. We watched as their relationships continued to develop. He was starting to talk about girls more frequently at dinner. He also started to become very opinionated about school, people, what is fair and unfair, and his siblings. He increased his joking with Tracey, working very hard to get her to turn red or get defensive. Always with a serious face, he would make a comment and stare at her. He started doing it to his sister as well. Logan and I wouldn't have any of it. He quickly learned to leave us out. He started going to movies and the mall with his "peeps" or "fam." He always needed money to fund his activities. So much so that Tracey decided he needed to go on an allowance of $100 a month to teach him to budget.

Maverick and Logan's relationship changed around this time. Instead of competitors, they became collusive. Logan at nineteen was stable with a job, school, his music, girlfriend, and his motorcycle. Logan started making more time for Maverick. They would play video or application-based games, sucking me in as well. They weren't arguing at the dinner table as much. They became our entertainers by breaking out in jokes, witty dialogue, dance, and opinions about current events. Their opinions became more aligned. They would partner against us during our Saturday night family games and compete fiercely. Maverick was actually listening to Logan's advice. Logan has always been protective of Maverick as well as all of us to some degree. We were seeing his protection on the surface. Maverick was rapidly becoming his friend and partner.

The end of the freshman year presented Maverick with two big shocks. The first was his grades. I tracked all our children's grades and assignments at least weekly on the school websites. They all know that education is extremely important to us. Maverick suddenly realized that just listening, taking the quizzes, and doing the homework would not ensure good grades. You have to actually read the material, study for the tests, be prepared for pop quizzes, do well on the projects, and pay full attention in class. He was very close to getting three "C"s going into the finals. I was all over him. He ended up with only one C but wasn't too happy with my threats to take away his phone (seemingly surgically connected to his hand) and his video games as well as my threat to constantly review his homework. My walks in the dark were all about asking for God's guidance to motivate him and keep him on the path.

The second shock, similar in nature, came when he went after his driver's permit. He knew the exact day he could take the test. So Maverick did the usual thing. He skimmed the book even though we told him to take practice tests online and really study the book. He walked in full of confidence only to fail within ten minutes. He had to wait seven days before taking the test again. Initially, he said he wasn't going to do it. Then suddenly he had a whole new attitude that we believe was brought on by his friends. He practically memorized the book. He passed the second time and wanted to drive right away. Prayers sorta answered.

Having a driver's permit changed Maverick. He quickly figured out that being a chauffeur "on call" gave him driving time. He started going to the gym with Tracey and found he liked to lift weights. He was taking more frequent store runs with her. Between us and the boys, we were spending close to $550 a week to keep food in the refrigerators (garage and kitchen). Five gallons of milk a week, really? I would take him out on Saturday and Sunday to drive and parallel parking practice. It gave us chances to have extended talks and listen to music together. He reminded me of my rule "he who drives also controls the tunes" and ultimately introduced me to a whole new set and genre of music.

As his skills grew, he got cocky. He pushed the speed limit, acted like stop signs were just a suggestion, and rode up too close to people. Never felt fear, but had to be alert sitting next to him.

Our trip to Colorado that year was a great time. Maverick was going through his third growth spurt, and he was working out regularly. We all took notice of his height and breadth. He had a "girlfriend" even though we forbid our children to date until sixteen. He was confident, charming (Logan called him a "player"), and entertaining. Quick to smile and say, "Hi." He had the looks, smarts, social skills, and the style; and he started using them to his full advantage. We went to Estes Park with my mother-in-law. We got our old time picture and then separated into Estes to shop. Maverick grabbed me to go to a store called "Lithium." Basically a young person's shop with all kinds of posters, shirts, paraphernalia, loud music, and basic teen counter culture stuff. We spent a whole hour going through the store with him giving me opinions on everything. I remember thinking that just a couple of years before he thought this store was "stupid and boring" and now it really has his attention.

Maverick spent the rest of the summer having sleepovers, going to sleepovers, hanging with his friends at the mall, working out with Tracey, and eating like two people. Every once in a while, he and/or Logan would go rattlesnake hunting with me in the desert.

Sophomore Year

In August 2015, my work responsibilities took me to Kauai. The boys were older and pretty self-sustaining as long as the refrigerators were full, so Tracey went with me. The boys were given strict lists and rules to follow. Logan had to take Maverick down to the high school to pick up his schedule and books, watch the dogs and cat, and no sleepovers. Sigh. Two out of three were followed. Found out after we got back that both boys had female visitors. We constantly texted the boys and sent them pictures from Hawaii. Maverick responding frequently commenting how pretty it is and how he would like to take surfing lessons one day. The home was a little messy when we arrived, but the boys were okay and the animals were okay. The visitor thing became a one-way discussion that ended with "our house, our rules."

Maverick turned sixteen in September. He started badgering us earlier that month about wanting a car. When he realized that we were not backing down from our "eighteen and graduating or a viable reason that you need one" rule as we had three cars that would be made available, he turned toward wanting a TV even though he had a huge HD multi-pixel thing in his room attached to all his different gaming systems. Tracey recorded an argument between them  over his "birthday wants." Maverick in lawyer mode and Tracey not backing down had me laughing and shaking my head at the same time. He ended up with a lot of expensive clothes and gift cards for clothes that made me wish I bought the car or the TV. Would have been cheaper.

The weekend before Thanksgiving, Maverick had calculated exactly when he could take his driver's test based on the date he obtained his driver's permit. He put together his argument that he should be able to take it the day after Thanksgiving. I told him that DMV would be closed. I got run over again. He had already had that data. He insisted I call on Monday and set an appointment for Friday. I think Tracey actually made that happen. Tracey, Maverick, and I showed up for his scheduled appointment on Friday—Tracey and I very nervous, Maverick calm and confident. He was using the car he had the most experience in: My relatively new Honda Civic Hybrid. The first test was parallel parking. He nailed it first time and looked at us with a big smile. Off he drove with the officer. Fifteen minutes later, he was parked out front talking with the officer. He smiled, nodded, and parked the car. The moment he came out of the car is etched in my brain. We knew. He smiling and doing a little happy dance, and us walking over to give him a hug. Our little boy is growing up fast.

Maverick wanted to drive right away and all the time. My car became Dad *and* Maverick's car. He was always going somewhere with his friends. He had increased his workouts in intensity and frequency. He started working out with Zoe, a rodeo barrel-racing cowgirl and wing-girl to Maverick, at least four times a week. After seeing them together a few times, we realized that their interactions were setting a foundation for a close relationship coming in the next few years. Both were dating other people, but Tracey and I agreed, during our Saturday state park walks, to keep an eye on them and to get to know her parents. Maverick was also constantly going out to late-night movies or fast food runs with his best friend, Ben and/or Andrew. He was buying clothes and eating his way through his monthly $100 allowance within two weeks. I started giving him money on the side for his food trips only. We would fist bump and man-hug swear that neither of us would tell Mom.

As Christmas approached, Maverick, Logan, and I took to putting the lights up in the yard and drive. A six-hour ordeal and fraught with perils. Putting up Christmas lights on four acres of cactus may seem counterintuitive to some, but all us boys know Tracey has expectations. Maverick and I pulled all the boxes out of the storage room in the two-car garage. We checked each of 150 strings of lights. Maverick suddenly had a special request. In our entry area, right outside his room, is a tree. He outlined a specific way it was to be decorated so that he could see it from his windows and his friends would all think it is cool. Took me two tries to get it right, but he was happy with the results and praised me for it. Tracey was very pleased with the work we did. She made a video and posted it on Facebook.

Around Christmas break, Maverick started his fourth growth spurt. He also dramatically changed his diet. He was drinking protein-based drinks, amino-based energy mixtures, muscle milk, and large amounts of water and Gatorade. He was eating four or five full meals a day that were protein based. Diet and growth spurt combined with workouts changed him. He was taller than all of us and far stronger in four short months. His confidence, backed by his size and growing social standing, was also increasing. He was honing his comedic skills with us at the dinner table almost every night. Grades were still a frequent talk point as was his need for the car to fuel his social interactions. He and Tracey had taken to watch movies together now and again. She lamented, while on our weekly walks, that she was seeing less of him since he was driving himself everywhere.

There are some things you need to know about Tracey. She is very, very much a mother. Has been since I met her. Mothered me until we had children. That quick change of my status was a shocker for me, but my dad warned me it would happen. I got over it. Mostly because she told me to get over it. She is also a collector. Once she gets her mind on something that captures her interest, then she dedicates herself to it. Whether it is Disney pins, Build-

a-Bear, Vermont Teddy Bears, a particular type of gem, refrigerator magnets, and wind chimes. Once she wanted to collect it, it was over. All of us in the house realize that about her.

So in the spring, when she started talking about walking labyrinths, we boys knew what was next. I spent a weekend designing and building a labyrinth in our front yard. I completely messed up the spacing and the walking paths were only six inches wide. I enlisted Maverick the next day.

He and I spent three hours completely re-laying out the paths. I was grateful for his size and stamina. We got wind chimes with solar night lights and built an entry walk close to our front door. He was very proud of the result. Tracey praised us for the effort.

The day after Mother's Day started out normal for Tracey. Maverick got off to school via his girlfriend. She put our two dogs out in the backyard to relieve themselves. She went out less than ten minutes later and couldn't find Ziggy, our yorkie. Our cocker, Pepper, fifteen years old and deaf, was wandering around, oblivious to everything. Panic calls and texts. Panic searches around the house, yard, and property. We all did a search of the property after the boys were home from school and I back from work. Maverick and I walked one portion of the property. Logan and his

girlfriend walked another. Our only conclusion is that an owl or hawk took him. Tracey was devastated. Maverick was devastated that it happened and how upset it made Tracey.

Two weeks later was the last week of school. Maverick was again borderline between Bs and Cs in three classes. He started  working on studying. Unfortunately, Maverick caught a very nasty bout of bronchitis, complete with fever, wheezing, cough, and fatigue. He would catch something like this about every three years. The timing was terrible. He had to stop his weightlifting diet, stop working out, use a steroid nebulizer, and take day time cold medicine just to get through finals. He was exhausted. He had just broken up with his girlfriend, found out one of his friends was starting to date an ex-girlfriend who he was discussing reuniting with, and most of his friends were going out of town on vacation right after school let out.

The last week of school, Tracey and Logan came home with Ruffles, a year old energetic cocker-poodle mix. Ruffles came from a home without children and was kenneled a lot, so he immediately  took to our two boys and the amount of activity in the house. Tracey took a great video of Ruffles and Maverick playing with an empty water bottle. Two kids playing. Ruffles would wait outside Maverick's door or Logan's door for them to get up so he could play.

The next week, Maverick was feeling healthier, but not well enough to work out and stayed off his workout diet. We had made an agreement with him that if he got a job, then we would buy him a car to get back and forth. He insisted that it *not* be a "POS" (piece of s——). Realizing the opportunity, Maverick started looking for a job. He focused on Tilly's and wouldn't look anywhere else. He liked the store and knew the layout since he was in there all the time. He put in online applications. He got an interview two weeks later.

On our walk that next weekend, Tracey and I chatted about the kids. But Maverick became the center of our discussion. Tracey was worried and presented her concerns. He wasn't working out. No friends around. Not active and was at times behaving at 80 percent of his normal self. He was eating pretty well and still chatting with us at dinner, but Tracey's mother instinct was on fire. We decided we would keep a closer eye on him and ask his brother and sister to do the same. He had been spending more time with his sister and her boyfriend's brother recently, so they might know something. We engaged him in multiple conversations about walking with us at the park, what was going on with his friends, and getting back to working out. Productive discussions and viable answers, but no real change in behaviors. We set our annual trip to Colorado for three weeks later.

He had his Tilly's interview and was told they would contact him "in about two weeks." He was thrilled. His friends were all coming back to town and his social interactions started increasing. Maverick went on a road trip with his best friend Ben the next weekend. He seemed to be doing better but texted us a couple of times

that he wanted to come home. He missed Sunday family dinner and apologized. He came home late and tired, but interacted with Tracey for a while before going to bed.

The next week, I traveled to Texas for a work event. Logan and Maverick had a bit of an altercation while I was gone. In a move to get him active again, Logan got Maverick to commit to doing some yard work with him. When Maverick tried to back out of his part of the deal, Logan took his phone until Maverick did his part of the job. When complete, Logan gave him his phone back. Words were exchanged, but our two boys settled it, bro-hugged, and ended up watching a movie together with Tracey. I came home late Friday to a calm house. Tracey told me all about the altercation on our walk in the park the next day. She also relayed that she was still worried about Maverick and detailed her concerns as well as details about his behavior. He seemed better to her, but something was still not right.

That night, we took Maverick to a local Mexican food restaurant. My head full of the altercation he had with Logan and Tracey's concerns voiced earlier that day, I started to engage him about the details of his current situation. He politely answered my questions and had reasonable explanations for his current behavior. I noted he didn't order as much to eat, and I asked him about it. He explained that he had eaten something earlier. I let it simmer until we were done and handed Tracey the keys.

Tracey went into the car, and I squared up with Maverick. A tense conversation in which I told him I didn't buy it. He wasn't eating, not working out, and not at the same level of social interaction with his friends unlike a mere three weeks before. He defended himself with the same answers as at dinner and told me I had nothing to worry about. I told him he was very close to me calling a counselor to sort all this out and asked him if he thought we (as a family) needed one. He told me an emphatic, "No, you are making way too much of this!" He got back in the car asking Tracey why I was getting on him.

The next Monday, the day before my birthday, we had our normal family dinner. Tracey and I were both tracking Maverick. He excitedly informed me that his wing-girl's, Zoe, birthday was coming up on Thursday, June 16. She loves dream catchers. I asked him if he needed money to buy one for her. He said, "I have a bunch in my old room. I want to give her those."

I cocked my head and said, "All of them, really?" We negotiated and settled on five or six that he thought she would like. I told him how to protectively wrap them. He was excited to give them to her and mentioned she would be very excited. I remember saying, "You sure you two are 'just friends'?" He asked his mother for wrapping paper and went to work.

My fifty-sixth birthday. Tuesday, June 14. The family was over to sing, cake/candles, and gifts. Maverick was back to his old self. He teased Tracey and Brenda. He and Logan partnered up on witty dialogue. I was happy to see the old Maverick back.

I got off work early the next Friday. It was date night and I had a birthday coupon from a local steakhouse. I checked the mail and found a statement from the bank for my daughter. I called and chatted with her for about fifteen minutes about how things were going and her job. Good conversation.

I decided to go to Logan's room and catch him before he went to work. We chatted about our upcoming annual trip to Colorado, his work, and some music stuff. Reminded him that Father's day was just two days away. Good conversation.

I went into Maverick's room next. He was sitting on his couch watching TV. I noticed his bed was made and room was cleaned. Not rare, but unusual. Ah, but the laundry basket was full of dirty clothes. I praised him for the room and asked why. He explained that Andrew was coming over to spend the night. He needed the car by six thirty to go get him. We spent the next twenty minutes chatting. I asked him if he wanted to go to dinner with us. "No, I don't like that place." Told him I would do his laundry in the morning if he took it down to the laundry room. Asked him how Zoe liked the dream catchers. We talked about Father's Day coming up and he laughed, saying, "I have a whole day to get you something." I apologized about the thing outside the restaurant and told him that we were just concerned parents. He smiled with "Yeah, I know." We then talked about the upcoming Colorado trip, him getting back to workouts, and what the next two years would mean for him, "The best two years of your life are the next two." He said, "That sounds real cool, Dad." Good conversation.

Tracey and I left for dinner an hour later. I told Maverick good-bye, and we would be home by about six fifteen so he could have the car. He said, "Okay. Have a good dinner." Tracey told him goodbye and started walking toward the front door. He called out to her and asked for a hug. He walked to the front door with her as I already had the car out front. He said, "Should I lock it?" Tracey said, "Yes." They exchanged "I love you" and she came out to the car. All the way to the restaurant, I told her about my conversations with our children. I told her that I thought Maverick was back, had plans for the evening, and told me he would be starting his workouts next week. We went into the restaurant.

CHAPTER 2

"WE LOST OUR SON"

DINNER WAS NICE. WE EACH had our regular favorites. It was a warm Arizona summer day. Tracey and I talked about family finances on the way home. We circled back on topics related to each of our three children. Brenda, jobs and money. Logan, school and selling his motorcycle. Maverick, recent bout of laziness but how he cleaned his room that day.

We arrived home at 6:24 p.m. Tracey and I got out of the car at the same time. I grabbed my iPad and Tracey grabbed her take-home leftovers. We walked through the door of the RV garage into the two-car garage heading toward the door to the house. The back of the garage has three small rooms: sewing room, storage area, work-out room. The workout room door was always open and the others always closed with the lights off.

Tracey was rounding her car, five steps away from the door to the house, and I was six steps behind her. Tracey noticed that the light was on in the storage room (the light was coming through under the door); she said she wondered why it was on and immediately said Maverick may have been getting wrapping paper for Zoe's gift the other day and left it on. Thinking nothing of it, I said I would get the light.

I turned and looked at the door. Looking down, I saw blood under the door and said, "What the hell is this?"

Tracey said, "What?"

I said, "It looks like blood."

She said, "Is it Ziggy?"

I opened the door until it was blocked and in a moment took in the scene. Laying partially on his side, blond hair cut in a "cool" style, clothes I recognized, a rifle I recognized, a very large pool of blood. I said, "Oh, God. No, it's Maverick." I turned toward her to block the scene. I saw a sight I will never forget. The look on the face of a mother, my wife, realizing her child is dead. Tracey pointed at me, screaming, "I told you, I told you, I told you."

I quickly closed the door and told her to get inside, I got this, and to call our children. She went inside screaming. Ruffles was barking. My mind went blank and super clear all at the same time. I put my iPad down and opened the door again. Careful not to disturb the scene or touch the blood, I leaned down over him and checked his pulse on his neck. Nothing. I checked the pulse in his right arm. Nothing. I checked the pulse on his right inner thigh. "Frick, nothing." I kneeled down and partially turned him toward me, reaching around his neck to make sure I wasn't getting a pulse. I prepared to resuscitate. I looked at his face; the chill up my spine told me my son was gone. I wouldn't be finding a pulse or be able to resuscitate. I gingerly laid him back and closed the door.

Tracey came out of the house barreling toward me and the closed door. I hugged her and held her back saying, "We have lost our son. He's dead." Told her she can't see him, go in, and call our children. She went back in. I stepped back into the room, patted his chest, and stroked his hair saying, "Oh, God, Maverick, I can't fix this. Why, my son?" I stepped out and carefully closed the door.

I pulled out my cell phone and called 911. It was six twenty-eight. I clearly and calmly told them my name, address, and that my wife and I had just come home from dinner to find my son dead from what appears to be a self-inflicted gunshot. She said the police were on their way, stay on the line until they arrive, she was going to put me on with medical. I said, "Okay, but he has no pulse."

I went back into the room, gripped his arm, and said, "Goodbye, Maverick. I love you. We all love you." I turned and closed the door with a focus of a man on a mission. I saw the open gun case in front of Tracey's car with the screwdriver he used to break the locks. He never used this weapon, so how did he figure it out? I froze for a second and medical came on the phone. He asked me four questions. As I was answering, I saw the first officer coming up the drive.

The first officer was a calm young man. I told 911 the police are here, which he confirmed through dispatch. I hung up. The officer asked me to show him the situation. I took him to the door, opened it, and said, "This is my son Maverick" as if he was alive. I turned away to see two other officers coming down the drive. It was six thirty-six.

The rest of that night is a blur to me. Moments of extreme clarity and others of foggy conversations.

I remember talking and texting to my father, my brother, my boss, my sister, a co-worker whose son knew Maverick, and Ben's dad, who works with me. I remember talking to my daughter. She said she just got a call from Mom and couldn't understand her. "Squirrel, come over right away. Maverick is dead." I told the officers to protect the scene and not let my wife near the room. They both nodded knowingly as they had just come from the room.

The police officer in charge asked to see his bedroom. He took one look around saying, "Is it always this clean?"

I said, "Not particularly. He just cleaned it today. My wife and I both praised him for it."

He looked at the closet and said, "He has a great selection of clothes. My kids would love having something like this." The officer picked up Maverick's phone and took it. He asked me to step outside and that they would have more questions. I told him I had questions myself. I went with him after a quick check with Tracey on the way out. He said that one or two detectives would be showing up momentarily.

The detective went straight to the storage room. I wasn't allowed in the garage at that point. "Active crime scene" was what I heard. I reminded the officers not to let my wife in or see the door open. The detective came up to me saying she had questions. In our basic discussion, she asked where Maverick got the gun and ammo. Not thinking about it before, I suddenly had the same question. The gun was stored in a locked case in the room where he shot himself. The ammo was tucked away in a back corner of our bedroom walk-in closet. She said she wanted to see the closet.

The sight upon turning the corner into the walk-in closet stunned me. The closet, at least my section of it, was completely torn apart. My shirts were tossed on the floor, all my hunting gear laid out, all my gym bags (where I stored ammo) were laid out in a neat row and open with ammo boxes laid out, and all my guns (mostly .22s) were lined up. She quietly said, "He was determined and very methodical." I pointed to an open box of .30-30 shells and said he was after that. One shell was missing from the full box. A week prior, purely as a fluke, I had moved all the ammo. I had resorted it, putting some in gym bags because I would probably never have a use. I had tucked the .30-30 ammo in a gym bag in the back corner of the closet. My heart fell as I realized he frantically searched until he found it. I thought he must have checked it out before, rehearsed, and that is why he tore things up. I left the room with a mental note to clean it up before Tracey had a chance to see it.

Met my daughter Brenda before she went into the house. She was in complete shock. I met my son Logan on the driveway. Hugging him and said, "He's gone, he's gone."

The police officer showed me Maverick's phone and said, "This is your son's phone. We are done with it. There are notes on it to multiple people that you will want to read."

I said, "You will need to get your techs to unlock it for me. I don't know his passcode."

He said, "No passcode. It was taken off two hours ago. Just swipe across." I read part of the first note to "family" (Dad, Mom, Brenda, and Logan), and realizing I couldn't handle it, I gave the phone to Tracey. She read all the notes. The notes were warm, friendly, well written, and made clear that he had been planning this for at least five days. She sent each recipient's parents his note to them.

My boss called me back to tell me that the company was informed and everything was in order. I was to contact him if I needed anything.

The officer in charge asked me if I needed anything, and I said, "Three hours back, but I guess you can't do that." And then I pulled out Maverick's wallet saying, "Yes. Here is his driver's license. Maverick is an organ donor. It is very important to him. Please tell the ME or tell me who to call." He took the license and walked over to the ME.

The "comfort" people came. A good group of people but really had no idea what we were going through at the moment. I remember thinking, "They are telling me how I feel and what I am thinking like they know us. They don't have a clue." I walked back outside. The detective gave a receipt for the gun saying I could have it back in two weeks or have it destroyed. She also gave me a package of information about funeral homes, reclamation services, community counseling services, and churches. She said words that froze me, "This is an obvious case of planned suicide. I am sorry for your loss. You and your family are clear." She left. I wanted to cry, but I couldn't.

The ME was done after about two hours. I told the ME what I thought had happened. She confirmed everything I suspected based on an image now frozen in my mind. Reiterating Maverick's desire to be an organ donor was received with affirmation that she had already called and emailed the appropriate groups. I suggested she put his arms up over his head before securing him. She agreed and told me to come back out in fifteen minutes. Brenda had left earlier. This whole scenario was obviously too much for her. I brought Tracey and Logan out to say goodbye to Maverick. It was ten thirty.

I decided to clean the mess on the garage floor and the floor of the storage room before Tracey had a chance to see it again. The entire storage room was a mess. Logan came out asking what I was doing. I told him to go back in and take care of his mother. The look in his eyes and his tone told me he wasn't leaving. I didn't argue. He was my rock. I remember saying to myself, "I am going to have to reevaluate my definition of Logan. He is way tougher than I already thought." We spent an hour cleaning the floor talking about being in shock.

I sat down at my computer and wrote a note to my staff telling them the basics of what happened and that I would be out for a while. Tracey was reading aloud the responses from his friends' parents. Everyone was stunned. So were we.

I organized the walk-in closet, and we went to bed around midnight. I slept in twenty- to thirty-minute spurts always waking to Tracey, holding my hand and crying. I hurt for her; I hurt for me and miss him. Images swirling through my brain. Wondering what would become of us. I have a hole in my heart, but she has a hole in her very soul. Tracey and I, laying in a bed of her tears.

Maverick died less than five miles from where he was born.

Maverick, what have you done, son?

CHAPTER 3

THE JOURNEY STARTS

I GOT OUT OF BED around 3:00 a.m. Tracey seemed to be sleeping. I decided to take our dogs for a walk. I usually took our fifteen-year-old deaf and very slow cocker (Pepper) walking on the quarter-mile section of the street and then came back to take Ruffles on the three-quarter section of the street. Took them both twice since the activities of the previous evening probably had them both stressed out. I came back for Ruffles. He was always at the door waiting for his turn. Not there this time. I looked down the hall and saw him on the  throw rug outside Maverick's door. He wasn't moving. I called to him, and after about thirty seconds, he slowly came to me. Very sad moment for me. Ruffles had lost his friend. Then I realized Ruffles probably followed Maverick through the house and heard the gunshot. With tears in my eyes, I took him out for our walk.

My mind was swirling. The events the night before pressed on my head. I circled around the question of "Why?" multiple times. Searched my memory for anything I did, should have done, could have done, and would have done differently. Tears were streaming down my face. I got to the cul-de-sac at the end of our street, stopped, and looked up. I said out loud, "God, I am not angry at you. You didn't do this. You probably tried to stop him. I know we can't have him back. I also know you have him. As his father and a man of faith, I have expectations that I pray you to honor. Take him to heaven and let him have the peace and happiness that he must have been seeking. Please help Tracey and Logan. You know they are so close to him. Help me figure out what to do." Music has always been a foundation of my life. Threads of sound that weave into the tapestry of my life. That very moment, I heard James Taylor singing in my head,

> Won't you look down upon me Jesus you've got
>   to help me make a stand
> You've just got to see me through another day
> My body's aching and my time is at hand
> I won't make it any other way
> I've seen fire and I've seen rain
> Seen sunny days that I thought would never end
> I've seen lonely times when I could not find a
>   friend
> But I always thought that I'd see you again

Knew I had to keep it together.

I put in my head that I needed to look at this just like a work project. I am a businessman. I can do this with two brains. One that is upset, but the other must stay on task. They would be in constant conflict. I started making lists of all the things I needed to do. Needed to make sure we set everything up with honor. Funeral home, work insurance for counselors, find church for funeral, make sure funeral is a celebration of his life and not his end, contact his friends, organize Maverick's room, and call the reclamation service for the storage room. Needed to make sure Tracey is happy with each part of the plan. Her child, her loss, her rules. Need to pulse Logan for ideas and to make sure we are not doing anything esoteric. Check with Brenda. I started lecturing Maverick as if he was walking next to me. Angry. The lectures and tears subsided by the second walk around the block. I was starting to focus. Well, as best I could.

I got into the house, wrote my initial to-do list, and ate a very small breakfast. Not hungry. Checked my work email. Read the nice notes and promises of help and support. I decided to read Maverick's note to us.

> Family
> I don't have individual messages to you guys because you were all so wonderful to me. Brenda with your acceptance and kindness, Logan with your helpfulness and wit, Dad with your paternal and charismatic instincts, and Mom with your constant selflessness and love. I want you all to know that I loved you all and this was not your fault. I promise it was not. Nothing you said or did caused this; if it was that I would've asked for a therapist of some kind to sort through problems that we had. It was not though. I had a poison in my mind that I could not get out that just grew and grew. No matter what I did or anyone else did there was no shaking this poison. It is not the only reason why I did what I did but it was the beginning of it all. Everything else just kind of added up. At first the idea of doing this was a small dot in my brain. If I got upset at something or stressed out I would think about doing it. Then it grew in my mind rapidly. Thinking about doing it turned into planning it, looking around the house, searching things online, etc. i can't help but think of how much of a waste I am, you guys put up with me, cared for me, talked to me, paid of me, and on top of that you loved me, and I threw it all away. I'm sorry, none of you deserved this in your life. I love you all; please just be happy without me.

Whoa. I got angry again. "Please just be happy without me." What the hell does that mean? This isn't the Maverick we knew and loved.

Work had given me some training. I have an executive coaching certification and have periodically filled my free reading time with behavioral psychology topics of interest. I turned this part of my brain to reading all about teen suicide, teen depression, and impact to survivors on the internet. Searched my brain for examples of his behavior as it relates to all the lists of warning signs. Two were a stretch and the rest meant nothing to me. Read the survivor elements and took note of key things: Grieving competitions and misunderstandings are the driver for divorce, siblings will hide their grief, memorials, "letting go," impact to friends, denial, anger, PTSD. I was consuming information at a rapid rate. I was angrily searching. How did he put this past me? How did I not figure it out? What did I do wrong here?

Tracey got up moments later. The sun had come up, and I didn't even notice. She and I decided to take a walk. We ended up walking for two and a half hours. As we were able to understand later, we were discussing all the standard "why"; "would've, could've, should've"; "who's to blame"; and "what now" questions in a muddy mixed blur through our tears. We would attack those methodically later. But our first walk set the foundation for how we would approach this as individuals and as a couple. She made me promise that I would not "shut down" and/or close her out. I have kept my promise.

The First Memorial

The next several days were a fog. His many friends sent us pictures, videos, and video tributes. Things we hadn't seen before. They showed our happy-go-lucky Maverick in entertainment and trouble-making mode. We cleared out his room, taking everything we wanted to keep. We allowed his closest friends to come over with their parents and pick things out. Logan and I found pot in his room. I quizzed Logan about it as Tracey and I thought this was completely incongruent to the child we knew. Logan told us where he thought Maverick got it, and I made a mental note to deal with that later. Reclamation service came and cleaned the storage room. We searched Maverick's phone and carefully kept all his text trails.

Flurry of phone calls, emails, and texts. My brother, David, and sister-in-law, Janine, were scheduled to come later that week. My best friend from work, Brad, and his wife were coming out. They had lost their youngest son to similar circumstances just three years before. His insight was and still is extremely helpful. My sister, Beth, and her boys would be at the funeral. Tracey and I were still in "why" and "who/what to blame" on our walks, but we were both rapidly reading up. She broke me from using the term "committed suicide" (very offensive to a grieving parent) and instead use "died by suicide." We started taking a hard look at our own perceptions, those placed into us by society and religion, about suicide.

Tracey and I found a great, caring, and empathetic funeral home. The director is a young woman who quietly comforted us and led us through paperwork, options, and costs. During our first meeting, Tracey started acting confused and upset. Turns out she was concerned about cost, making a mistake, and making wrong choices surrounding keepsakes. Would we cremate him or have him buried? I called a timeout and took her outside. I summarized my feeling about her concerns, "Baby, he is our son. But you are his mother. My role is secondary. Our son, our loss, and your rules. Cost is not an issue. You will get what you want and whatever you want to have happen, I will make happen." She said something like, "Just make sure I don't do anything that is weird."

We met with a church Tracey had attended. The pastor was very nice and the church had advanced audio-visual setup. We decided to make the funeral the next Saturday. The rest of the week the pastor, funeral director, and I worked through the details behind the "Maverick: A Celebration of Life" show.

Tracey and I continued our research about Maverick, teen suicide, and grief. No real plan. More like data gathering. Zoe's stepmom, Jessie, gave us a great book about loss that got us started. She and her husband, Sean, are Maverick fans. Brad had a book sent to us as well. Our discussions on our walks were more linear and chronological. A couple for over twenty-five years and grieving parents, we naturally divided research and used our walks to compare mental notes, assumptions, and feelings. Tracey had all the Maverick research well under control and was interacting with his friends with questions. I summarized in a concept of a huge "Maverick Paint-by-Number Mural" that I ended up writing and sharing with others nine months later.

Maverick Mural

In the beginning of our grief journey, I felt like Tracey and I were presented with a huge, partially complete paint-by-number mural of our Maverick. Little tiny spaces with numbers on them and a box full of paints, his life details, with numbers. We set out painting the empty spaces. We started realizing the box didn't have all the paints. We needed to go look for them. We would find a missing color only to discover that some of the other numbered colors changed with our discovery. Our perfect picture became discolored and unrecognizable. We had to clean off spaces and repaint. We kept at this for quite a while. There are still some little white spaces on the mural. We have tried to use the other paints, but it just doesn't make the picture a "work of art." So we keep searching even though we know we may never find them.

Less than a week after Maverick died, I also formulated a concept of "My Backpack." First presented to Tracey, Brenda, and Logan in my kitchen to describe my concept of survivor grief. I refined it on my walks. I wrote it and shared it with groups about nine months later as well.

The Backpack

The moment I found Maverick, I felt like God put a huge backpack on me. Stenciled across the back is the name "Maverick" in big, bold letters. It contains very heavy rocks. All my would've, could've, should've, wishes, memories, plans, and wants. It also had tiny helium balloons in them. All my great memories, smiles, laughs, his smile, his smell, his successes that we helped with, interactions I saw, and interactions I was a part of.

I take a rock or two (or three or four) out every day. I look at them, sometimes cry on them, and rub them in my hands. Over time I have been able to make them smaller. I know they will never go away. I take the balloons out too. Each time they get a little bigger. The backpack has slowly lightened.

In the first few months after Maverick, there were discoveries. Pictures, stories, and things we didn't know. They were also put in the backpack or actually made some of the rocks heavier. Sigh. Just have to get stronger.

MavMom has a backpack too ... and so does MavBro and MavSis. We sometimes show each other our rocks and helium balloons. We compare and comment on them. We find some are exactly the same and some are very different. We have learned not to criticize each other's rocks and helium balloons. We can't take the rocks away from each other, but we can help keep the helium balloons filled.

Some days the backpack is very heavy or adjusted such that a rock is poking me in the back. Those are tough days. I have learned to make adjustments. Luckily, there are others around that show or tell me how to adjust the backpack so as to ease my discomfort when I am struggling with it. I also know those are the days I need to care for the helium balloons or I will ultimately be crushed.

I have shown my rocks to others. They have tried to take them away from me, tell me they have similar ones, react to them like they are ugly, or say, "It's just a rock, throw it away." Some I used to call my friends and some were close family members. I don't show them my rocks anymore. They don't understand the reason of my rocks.

Some actually like to look at the rocks and really try to understand why I have them. I like those people very much.

Others have backpacks like mine. I know them without ever meeting or see it in their eyes before we ever speak. We talk about our rocks and balloons. We talk about ways to look at and work with our rocks to make them smaller and ways to increase the balloons.

So that is my backpack. I never wanted it. I prayed hard in the first week for God to take it off of me. I prayed that MavMom would have hers taken off. Now I pray that I have the strength to carry mine and the wisdom to lighten MavMom's.

We weren't eating much, didn't feel like preparing food, and sleeping only four hours a night on a good night. Neighbors, David and Janine, and my Cousin Kristi and her husband, Jerry, stepped in and got us food and prepared meals.

Reclamation of the storage room left a terrible chemical smell. I painted it and starting lighting incense in the room just to keep the garage from reeking. It was a start of a memorial. I knew it and didn't care. I went to the room every night before I went to bed and said, "Good night, son, I love you." This was my custom for the past five years. He would always say, "Good night, Dad. Love you too. Have a good day tomorrow." I missed his voice.

Maverick's funeral was an understandable emotional time. We had a slideshow of his pictures with music picked by Brenda, his videos, songs he wanted played, four of his friends prepared to speak, pall bearers selected, and the pastor prepared to direct the show. I had heard a song in my head on one of my walks earlier that week, "Forever" by Vertical Horizon, and chose to include it. I handwrote the words to it and was prepared to give it to Tracey at that point in the service. We made our way to the church. Everything was ready.

I wasn't ready to walk in and see my son's casket at the front of the church. I just stared at the blanket of white roses with the single red rose on top that was specifically put there for Tracey to have after the service. The slideshow of pictures and Brenda's music was playing. Blown-up pictures of him standing around his casket and altar. My heart dropped. I had a mini-panic attack and suddenly didn't want to be there. Tracey started crying, which snapped me out of it. David, Janine, Beth (my sister), Brenda, and Logan comforted her.

Our guests started arriving, and I decided that I would greet each one with at least a handshake, if not a hug. The church was full. Many of my work staff and peers were in attendance. Many of his friends from school were there. Young people that had been to our house many times. Brad, Sean (another close friend from work who flew in), David and Logan were watching over me and seating guests. I could feel their eyes on me. Tracey's friends, several of which had flown in, my sister, Janine and Brenda stayed with her.

The service went off without a hitch. The pastor spent a little too much time on "it's the devil's fault" line of lecture, a subject that he and I disagreed. Brenda later commented that she didn't appreciate Maverick's funeral being an advertisement for the church. Maverick's four closest friends gave heartwarming and sometimes humorous speeches and tributes to our son. We showed his videos and video tributes taken by his friends. People laughed at particular funny five-minute video we titled "Equals Awesome." Maverick is running through the high school, pointing things out and saying, "That's awesome" or "Equals awesome" while putting his thumbs up. Toward the end, Tracey and I sat next to other in disbelief. Later we both realized we had the same thought, "Maverick, if this is a joke, you got me. You can come out now."

We walked behind the casket, leaving the church. I held Tracey's hand. Bob Dylan's "Knocking on Heaven's Door" playing in my head. Logan, Cousin Nick, Andrew and Ben were his pall bearers. Tracey and I were numb. We walked all the way to the curb. The boys put him into the hearse. I just stared, saying to myself, "Goodbye, my son. I love you." I walked Tracey back to the entrance of the church through a crowd of people feeling completely blank. Our son is really gone. Knocking on heaven's door.

The Second Memorial

Tracey, Logan, and I climbed on a plane the next day. Brenda stayed behind for work and to take care of the animals. This trip was planned a month before as our annual trip. We had decided to sell my grandmother-in-law's (Luella) house we bought ten years prior. She had moved in next door at my mother-in-law's (Dottie) house.

The boys were going to follow us two days later and help with clean out. How things changed in a month.

It was hard for us to leave the house that morning. None of us wanted to leave without Maverick. This would be the first time in sixteen years we had been there without him. On the plane, Logan would have an empty seat next to him where his brother would either be chattering or sleeping. In addition, we knew we would have an emotional first meeting with all of Tracey's relatives. We arrived at my mother-in-law's, and after tearful greetings, we settled in. They had watched Maverick grow up, and like us, were visibly stunned. We went to my father-in-law's (Rod) and step–mother-in-law's (Nancy) house that night. Both big Maverick fans, we saw the sadness in their eyes. We discussed everything we thought we knew about Maverick's circumstances. With tears in our eyes, we sadly and collectively said, "We didn't get a vote." He quietly said, "I know."

Rod had set up for a memorial at his church. Pastor Michael would preside. A kind and empathetic man, he quickly understood what we wanted and what he would do. The church didn't have the same audio-video capabilities as the first memorial, so we would have to go with a slideshow and no videos. I got to work on a slideshow that emphasized our Colorado trips and family. Tracey, Dottie, and Rod set about letting the family members and Tracey's high school friends know the date and time. Dottie got an obituary put into the Loveland paper.

Also that same week, we dealt with the realtor, got Luella's old house cleaned up for sale (Dottie and Tracey coordinated a lot of it), and met with our financial advisor and friend, Matt Simmons, to discuss investments and anything we needed to know considering our change in life circumstances. We met Matt, as usual, at Johnson's Corner. A nice roadside truck stop place with a long history and great food that we frequented while in Colorado. I got tears in my eyes when we pulled up as I could see the boys walking inside just last year.

There were reminders of Maverick everywhere. Dottie's tree out front where he carved his initials. His handprints in concrete we laid several summers before. The pool table in Dottie's basement where he first beat me. All the local stores where I would take the boys to pick up things. Games after dinner were sadness triggers for me. We went to Estes Park and took an old time picture with Logan. We have decided that will be our last old-time photo. I stood and stared at the store "Lithium" for at least five minutes. Every corner I turned, he was there. The first morning, I walked in the assisted care community next to Dottie's property listening to my iPod. The song "Nutshell" by Alice in Chains came on. I froze and suddenly felt like a kid that just wanted to go home. I then heard "Adam's Song" by Blink-182. Felt like it was a message to get inside his head to really

understand what happened. All that trip, Tracey and I continued our walks and talking extensively about our theories. She seemed a little more at ease.

His second memorial in Loveland went off well. Pastor Michael was great and really knew what to say. I only choked up twice. Once when I saw Chris, my step–brother-in-law. We had been around him and watched him grow up over the years. The second time was when I saw Logan sitting by himself at the front of the church before the service. He just looked so alone, and I frequently checked on him. We decided to have food served after the service as many of Tracey's family and friends had traveled from other parts of Colorado and Nebraska. While eating, several of Tracey's cousins engaged us about their concerns. Signs to watch for and things that would cause this to happen in their lives. Tracey and I both walked away, making note that there is not enough education out there for parents.

Logan and I left for home the next day, July 3. Tracey stayed behind for another week. Logan went right back to work. I was in the house by myself for the first time on July 4. It was a very sad time for me. I spent a lot of time throwing the ball in the pool for Ruffles and thinking to myself. The rush of activity was done, and I was starting to decompress. I took long walks, researched, and hypothesized by myself. Sat in Maverick's room and wrote notes on my computer. There were phone calls with Tracey and family, but they didn't help. Tracey wasn't here for us to have a running dialogue on the spur of the moment. I chatted with Logan a few times, but his girlfriend was around a lot and I wanted him to focus on his life. I told the police department to destroy the gun. Talked to the ME's office about other questions that came to me. Didn't get any more information. Watched his videos with tears in my eyes. Made sure all was on track at the funeral home to pick up his ashes and special order remembrances. I finally decided to turn my sights toward going back to work.

Back to Work

I went back to work on Wednesday, July 6. Maverick had been gone for nineteen days. At this point, I was extremely grateful for all the research. Tracey was at the front of the pack. Her knowledge base was growing far beyond mine. She was a great source on which for me to bounce my ideas. I decided that I should address my staff and acknowledge the elephant that was now in the room. Actually, the elephant sitting on my shoulders. I asked the human resources people if they had any guidance. Having never come across this before, they put me in touch with the local Employee Assistance Program person. After being scolded for coming back too soon and patronized with all she "just knew" I would go through, I decided to create an address to my extended staff, I obtained HR approval. I pulled my staff together within an hour of my return and read them the following (cut down for here):

All,

It has been a tough several weeks for my family and me. Thank you for all the cards, prayers, and well wishes. We are grateful for all the support.

By now, all of you know that Friday, June 17, Tracey and I came home from a typical Friday date night to find our world shattered. We were rushing home, as usual, to let Maverick use my car for a "hang out" event with his friends he informed us of earlier.

The last two and a half weeks has been full of discovery … of ourselves, of our family, of our friends, of Maverick's friends, and of Maverick. Nothing really new, which has been a blessing and a curse. The person you may have seen in the videos is the person we had in our home.

My spouse, children, extended family, and I are experiencing one of the most extreme types of mourning anyone can experience. We have counselors found by Company Health Advocate, our family, and each other to help us work through our many, many questions.

We (my family, extended family, and me) are grieving. Maverick was three months shy of his seventeenth birthday and our youngest … four years junior to his brother, Logan. Hence, we had many future plans and processes in work that had "Maverick" at the core. All of us are just starting to identify and sort through all the changes we need to consider.

Grief takes many forms with very individualistic processes, duration, and intensity. It is hard to know what to say or do when a co-worker has suffered loss. I fully expect people to interact with me differently … and they already have.

Not a problem. Through all the discussions, company resources, external resources, support groups, and internal reflection, I have summarized some things that will help:

A) I am not fragile, won't breakdown, and won't "lose it."

B) I firmly believe people have the best of intentions. Saying nothing is okay. Saying "I am sorry" is perfectly fine. Asking about Tracey is fine. Here are things that have been said to me that may be true, but I would ask you to avoid as I don't react well:
  a. "He is in a better place."
  b. "God willed it" or "It was his time" or "He is in heaven now."
  c. "I understand how you feel because my ... passed away."
  d. "Time heals all wounds," "You will be fine in time," or "You will forget all this in time."
  e. "At least you have two other children."
  f. "It could have been worse."

C) People respond to different triggers when grieving. Has nothing to do with you, but a discussion, a word, an interaction, or an innocent comment may prompt me to
  a. get up and walk away;
  b. shut down or behave slightly, but noticeably, outside my norm;
  c. Note: I catch myself quickly and am good when it is mentioned to me;
  d. Note: mentioning Maverick's name, seeing his picture, asking about what happened (please don't press if I ignore),

or how I am doing does not cause any problems.

D) On thinking clearly. People who have gone through this have commented about having to function while half of their brain processing power is quietly devoted to elements of the grieving process. There are periods of time (when not processing grieving things) that I have extreme clarity only to slow for another period as my brain starts "back-room" processing yet again. Hence,

   a. I may ask you repeat things.

   b. I may not be able to recall something clearly.

   c. I will process to a conclusion very quickly and wonder why others aren't keeping up.

   d. I will seem to tune out for short periods (less than thirty seconds). Happens rarely and I am good when prompted.

   e. I may seem fatigued. Grieving is a huge drain on a person's physical resources.

E) Other work behaviors. According to all the resources and introspection, I will likely

   a. feel a great need and am expected to help Tracey and Logan adjust to the different home environment and life cadence. They had the most frequent interaction with Maverick and the void in their lives is very, very large. Especially for Tracey.

   b. have separation anxiety from Tracey, Logan, and my home. Likely will not want to travel over a period of time.

Have already felt this when Tracey, Logan, and I traveled to Colorado for the second memorial. We all had to force ourselves to leave the house.

c. change my arrival time, departure time, and amount of work I do on weekends. It is expected that I will increase my work time as it provides me a release, a distraction, stimulates me intellectually, and I have a great need for accomplishment/results.

d. I have been told my base behavioral makeup, and the fact that my protection mechanisms were so suddenly and strongly activated, will drive me to be extra protective of my co-workers and will take a very strong stand if I feel someone is being treated unjustly. Just call me on it.

e. When asked about Maverick or the situation, and if I choose to speak to you about it, then I tend to flow out a non-stop stream of things or babble. I usually catch myself when I do this. But, call me on it if I say something uncomfortable to you or haven't caught myself before your tolerance has run out. I have to live it; you do not. But I appreciate the interest.

f. I have a high sensitivity to everyone's nonverbal communication. Counselors have told me that I have high EI that has been put into overdrive through this situation and my great drive to protect my family. I have made people uncom-

57

fortable because I have just "read their mind."

g.   I don't stress and I don't panic. After the last several weeks, I have found that regular stressful things don't even vibrate my stress meter. Been told that this will probably be the case for the rest of my life. Just an expected change of perspective. I will be able to sense your stress level, but you will have to be clear with me about "urgency."

There were some bumps in the road and people running right into what not to say. But for the most part, my staff and peers settled in with me and me with them.

Tracey came home the next weekend. We were happy to have each other around and started right up on our talks and things we thought. We went to the funeral home in the next week. They had set up a really nice room with Maverick's urn and laid out all the things Tracey had picked out. We drove everything home talking about the best times to invite his friends over to pick up stuff we got for them. We hoped they liked what we picked out and would honor the ashes within. Ultimately, four of them did and still do, and are forever on our radar: Ben, Hannah, Tori, and Zoe. They are our adopted nephew and nieces. We will do anything for them.

We placed his urn on the fireplace mantel with a Maverick memorial picture book Hannah had made and other little treasures.

After twenty-six days, Maverick was home.

We miss our son.

Chapter 4

The Real Work of Grief

After Tracey got back from Colorado, things started settling down. The social demands of our situation subsided. We took multiple paths in search for information. One key path driven by Tracey, we became our own little detective agency and started really digging into Maverick's life. We were documenting texts, notes, and knowledge points in a chronological timeline that started with his last three weeks and went back eight months. Where we had gaps, we attempted to fill in with interviews of his siblings and friends. We augmented our information with behavioral, suicide, and depression research we were doing. Her more-than-me since I was back at work with my hands full. Another path was grief counseling. We had family grief counseling sessions. Tracey, Logan, and I also had separate sessions with other counselors. We pooled our knowledge points. Tracey started attending group meetings like "Compassionate Friends" and "Grief Share." She was picking up common themes and resource information. Finally, Tracey joined several private groups on Facebook that strictly dealt with suicide loss. This further solidified her "common theme" knowledge. She and I were sharing information back and forth.

Both Tracey and I felt a sense of urgency toward understanding what happened to Maverick. Once she gets ahold of something, she doesn't let go. I started as a guy along for the ride, but quickly became interested in her approach. Perfect combination of her creative thinking and my analytical bent. We documented his last three weeks and then expanded. Unknown friends, pretend friends, discussions about depression and about buying pot, who knew what and when, the females in his life and their interactions, and his basic mental state were all culled from the data. We frequently climbed into Maverick's head at a specific point in time attempting to assess his social, physical, mental, and emotional state. We researched what marijuana would do, what the change of diet would do, how stopping his workouts impacted his brain chemistry, impact of parental interactions, impact of sibling interactions, how his social nature would be shaken by the end of school and his friends leaving for early vacations, and the impact of teens when they break off a romantic relationship.

My walks in the dark helped. She would present a set of concepts that I would sometimes reject. I would then think about it on my walk and see her logic. We took a lot of walks together and sat on the couch for hours talking about all the information, pulling it together into something coherent. Along the way, we were grieving, each of us having mostly offsetting Maverick meltdowns that disrupted our processes. We confronted the danger of our research. Every new piece of information couldn't and shouldn't be used to paint or repaint the entire portrait of Maverick. We were not only searching for information, but also searching for blame. As normal for grieving parents, mothers more so, we frequently turned the blame on ourselves as individuals. We were his last line of defense. So where did we let him down? Would've, could've, should've in full bloom. We kept at this in earnest for a couple months until we concluded that we wouldn't have all the answers and wouldn't really know for sure. But we had 97 percent of the story. We still keep at it from time to time. It was in this period that Tracey said, "You have to forgive yourself for not taking action to correct something you knew nothing about and was never told." Wise words.

Counseling was helpful to some extent. We went through multiple counselors. After a couple of family sessions and a session with just Tracey and me, I was all done. I respected their education and experiences, but none of them ever lost a child to suicide or even close. In their defense, how many counselors really have to face a grieving family over the suicide loss of a child in their entire career? I had enough of the "textbook" talk. I was getting that info from the internet, and Tracey was far more versed. Telling the story only to be told how I should think and that I shouldn't blame myself bothered me. I found I was becoming argumentative having to defend myself and my conclusions. After multiple sessions, one frustrated counselor said, "You guys aren't going to get off the 'why' question, so I guess we will need to talk about it." I believe they were truly trying to help us. Just kept thinking they were telling me where to go on a map but hadn't tried to understand my current location, which left me without a direction. They did help us open up new avenues of thought and information trails to research, which Tracey and I discussed at length.

Tracey and I were carefully watching Logan. Logan was upset from the start that Maverick didn't come to him. They had developed a solid bond, and Maverick well knew that Logan would do anything for him. Logan felt disrespected, rejected, disappointed, and angry. Logan has been our honest child since he was a middle teen. You have to ask directly, but you will always get a straight answer. Just be careful what you ask because the answer will come out with little sugarcoating, if any. We didn't want to hover. We wanted to allow him his space. Yet we made sure to give him audience or probed if we felt he was processing Maverick.

The counseling sessions seemed to help. He was now starting to channel his grief in his music, songs, and poetry as opposed to bottling it in. He would play guitar for long periods. Very sad songs that we came to like to hear in the other room. His work and school didn't miss a beat. We were also glad to have him around during our hardest grieving period. He was frequently playing and singing a song he wrote called "Sad Soul." The first part of the song goes like this:

> I knew a sad soul
> But I didn't know his soul was sad
> I wish I would've known
> His soul was so prone to being sad
>
> Was it so long ago
> That you wore my clothes

My socks
My socks over your toes
And looking in your room
Knowing you wouldn't
Be there soon

Logan turned twenty-one in early August. He was put on anxiety medication and took himself off just two days later when he spent a night with suicidal thoughts. He later told Tracey that he fought off the impulse because "we have all gone through too much." He was able to buy alcohol and turned to it for relief of his pain. He pulled himself off of that as well. He still drinks too much from time to time when he is really upset about Maverick, but for the most part keeps himself under control. His girlfriend became more of a member of our household and keeps close tabs on him. Logan and I took up golf, played pool, played darts, and talked about going rattlesnake hunting again. We felt the vacuum of loss when we played games. Just wasn't the same without Maverick telling us "good shot," giving us grief about a bad shot and gloating when he beat us. College started, he was working, and his girlfriend was always around, so Logan settled down and our game playing was put on hold.

I was closely watching Tracey. I had work and was busy. I got away from the house, had intellectual interactions, and the expectations of my employer and myself allowed daily vacations away from "Grief Island."

Tracey was wrapping herself up in the Maverick research, grief groups, Facebook groups, and awareness reading every day. She got her first tattoo, of many, in honor of Maverick. A reproduction of the last words Maverick physically wrote on my birthday card. Brenda went with

her and eventually got a beautiful "Maverick Wave" on her right arm. Tracey and I were talking every night about her reading and discoveries. We had started back up on our Friday "date night" dinners. We went to some of the same restaurants. The servers have known us for years and knew what happened, so either or both of us crying at the table didn't cause panic. Plus, we had watched many of our servers grow up over the years and liked to find out the things in their lives. Still can't bring ourselves to go into Chilli's.

Tracey started down the "Memory of Maverick" and suicide awareness road around the time that Maverick's junior year started. A tough time for both of us. We went to his school the weekend before

it started and spread his ashes at all the places we had seen in the videos and pictures. Tracey started creating wristbands, created a MoM ("Memory of Maverick") movement and business cards we gave out when we secretly paid for a stranger's dinner, collected wind chimes, gathered and painted rocks for the labyrinth, got us all pictures of Maverick on screen prints and solid back frames, decorated her car (Maverick sticker on back and "MavsMom" license plate), and other assorted Maverick or awareness associated items. She got other tattoos. She was fixated on sunsets and rainbows that she knew would get Maverick's attention and felt he was sending to her/us. She tried to suck Logan and me into her activities and we would sometimes agree, but no tattoos for us.

The time leading up to Christmas held several turning point events for us. His seventeenth birthday was late September. We threw a party complete with cake, balloons that we released with notes and mini LED lights. Many of his friends and parents participated. We went to a high school football game to see his best friend, Ben, play. It was the first time we were on campus since before school started. Both of us were triggered by the students with similar haircuts, walk, and style.

We found out that a complete mix up occurred between the ME and the organ donation group the night Maverick died. The organ donation people admitted, on the phone and in a nice letter to us, that they completely "dropped the ball." Tracey was devastated and I was upset that our sixteen-year-old healthy weightlifter did not get a wish he actually fought me over less than a year before. We participated in the local "Out of the Darkness" walk. Tracey created "Team Maverick" that included friends and their families. We celebrated our twenty-fifth wedding anniversary in Las Vegas. We attended several shows and took a lot of walks. We could feel Maverick with us the whole time.

Tracey set up a candlelight memorial in memory of Maverick. Set as an awareness event at a local church, she put together a nice awareness document to present and asked me to write and speak. When it was her turn, Tracey got sucked into a "Maverick Loss" hole and asked me to present her material.

Tracey's speech:

> What can I say to get your attention?
> Because I need your attention
> I WANT your attention
> What can I do to make you listen?
> Because I need you to listen
> And not just listen to me
> I need you to hear me
>
> This is about AWARENESS

For you, for your friends, for your families
This is about SUICIDE

Let me tell you upfront and in your face
SUICIDE SUCKS!!
How do I know this?
Because 112 days ago I lost my youngest son Maverick
        Albert Campisi to suicide
He was 16
He will forever be 16
On the edge of 17
He never made it to 17
At least, not here on earth
I, along with many people he left behind, are devastated
As a mother, as HIS mom, as the person that gave him life
I am heartbroken
And I don't mean heartbroken like you broke up with a girl
        or a boy
I literally mean my heart can't be fixed
My world has changed
I have changed
Oh don't get me wrong, please
I'm still a wife to my husband Michael
A mother to my daughter Brenda Michelle
A mother to my son Logan Davis
I'm a daughter, a niece, a granddaughter, a sister-in-law,
and many call me "friend"
And yes
I am still Maverick's Mom
But a piece of my heart is forever gone now that he is gone

So where can I begin?
What is my message to you today?
What do I want you to HEAR or SEE from my experience?

First of all, unfortunately I can't save Maverick

But in my healing process, and to move forward in my
    grief, I have come to realize I
want to help others that may be suffering. I want to speak
    up and speak out
Because SUICIDE SUCKS and needs to be stopped
I look back at the signs in hindsight
Of course, we can find those easily on the internet
But don't let the internet fool you
Be aware of your own child. What's normal for them or not
    normal can open your eyes
to so much
There were only 1 or 2 things off with Maverick
But nothing more than normal teenage behavior
Or so I thought
And I should know, because I have been surrounded by
    teens for the last 12 years.
So has their normal behavior changed?
Do they seem off or different, or more quiet than usual?
Or louder and angry?
Ask them how they are.
And try this.... LISTEN to their answer.
Look at them and HEAR their answer.
Mostly my message is for anyone quietly suffering.
It is for that friend you know that mentioned they are feel-
    ing worthless or hopeless.
This is to ANYONE out there today that thinks they don't
    matter.
You DO!!

The hardest thing to cope with after losing Maverick is
    something called "the ripple effect".
This means what his death has affected with everything
    surrounding his life and what he
left behind
He left us with a million pieces to try to put back together

His friends, his family, his siblings, his teachers, his loved
     ones, his Mom and Dad.
We are all forever effected, forever changed, forever missing
     him
His pain is transferred to us

Another thing he left behind was his future
We will never know what he was meant to become, what
     career path he was meant to take.
We will never know whom he was meant to marry.
We will never meet the children he was meant to have.

So for you out there, yes you, that happy person on the
     outside, that struggling person
on the inside.
Tell someone you need to talk
Ask someone to listen
     Because we care!

We've taught you to tell us when your head hurts, or when your
stomach hurts, or when you have an injury, then why not tell us
when your mind doesn't feel right?

It's ok. It happens.
It's ok to talk about it
It's ok to raise your hand and say I think I need help
We as parents will do anything for our children
So talk to us
Or tell a friend
Or a teacher
Or another adult you look up to
Don't hide your feelings inside
There are many choices in life
There are ALWAYS choices
Don't choose suicide

Talk – Listen – Care
And
Be – Aware

Tracey L Campisi
10/7/16

All the events and activities marked us in different ways. But we were starting to see that we were becoming less internally focused. We were turning toward awareness and helping others cope with their losses.

After his birthday and before the candlelight awareness memorial, I started writing a poem. More of an open letter to Maverick from me. Formulated during multiple walks in the dark. Pieced together over a week's time from all I was thinking and feeling. I initially wrote it only for me. While at work, I suddenly had a feeling, a gnawing feeling that I needed to get it out. I pensively asked Tracey to read it.

Tracey has always been my muse. An extremely nonlinear and creative chatterbox with very well-honed social skills. Maverick got that from her. She is my source of constant intellectual stimulation and entertainment. Plus, she is the mother of my children. So I readily yield to her opinion. She gave it glowing praise and posted it to her page, Maverick's page, and some of her Facebook "grieving parent" groups. It received a terrific response very much to my surprise. I still think it testifies that I should stick to engineering and business management. Clearly shows that I went to the Dr. Seuss and Yoda School of Rhyme. Here it is in the original form.

Where are you, my son?
(A letter to Maverick)

Where are you, my son?
Is it a place you can dance?
Are there never ending rainbows and sunsets
In colors that entrance?
Is the music what you like?
Do the angels sing loud
or is it so soft that it brings hush to the crowd?
Do you have friends to joke and hang?
Talking in your own form of slang?
Is there food you like to eat,
Even if it only feeds your soul?
Is it a place you can rest in a bean bag seat?
A place you are glad to stay
A world of endless peace, happiness and play

Do you hear me say, "Hi, Maverick, it's Dad, I hope you're
      okay"
On the dark mornings of my walks?
And then see me look for a shooting star
To tell me you are?
My prayers for your peace
Are my greatest release

I am sorry for my continued lectures in the early morn
I sometimes get angry at you

I have expectations for all my children
From the time you were born
Things I worked for with your every breath:
Success, happiness, and love
That your past is a solid path of good things done
And that nothing can't be overcome
My anger turns when I think of your disarming smile,
     blond hair,
And how alone you walked your last mile

Do you hear me speak to you outside the door where you
     left?
I sit in that space and say you left for no reason
About your mom, sister, and brother:
The things they are up to, the change of season.
Always praying their grief leaves soon
Walking out with a choked voice in ruin
Straightening out before facing them in the other room

Or when like now all alone I wander into your bedroom
The place that was your protective shell
Just to remember our last talk
Just to remember your smell
Your consistent "good night love you too"
That told me all was well

I remember your blue eyes, your smile, and your infectious
     joy
In my dreams during the day
I remember your style, cutting your hair just so
Buying you the shirt you had to have
And doing your laundry to make it ready
For the night's events you always planned so steady

How at you and your brother the girls would stare
And how you would act like you didn't care

But surely taunt your brother with a dare
Giving you money out of cycle when you were low
We would both talk about how Mom would give us grief
We would conspire to make her laugh
Hoping she would give us relief

Your Mom sees you in sunsets and rainbows
You are so much like her
Seeing the beauty in the simple things, sensitive to others,
    quick to smile
The first to point out an unfair
She misses you so much
I worry sometimes if it is more than she can bare

Your sister and brother are working out their feelings of
    your loss
They watch Mom and I wrestle with all the questions that
    start with "Why"
Your brother sometimes burns hot,
And you very well know why.
He could have helped you,
Reach out to him you did not
You sister shields her loss too,
Wondering what would have become of you
I see you in the colors of her new tattoo

We see your friends now and then
In their presence I have peace
Their hidden sadness causes me to pause
You meant a lot and gave much to their lives and cause
For those times of you I am happy and proud
For their loss of you my soul screams aloud

Where are you, my son?
It's me, your father, your guide,
The one with no fear of you and nothing to hide

Just one of many that loves you
One who hopes you found a place of peace
Like my prayers requested
A place where your worries are erased
Like all my past words suggested
Where people all know your name
All the great things done
And how proud I am that you are my son

For now I have to leave your room
I have talked and typed enough
Oh, I will talk again to you soon
Until then I will carefully watch over
The other souls God entrusts to my care
And the memories of you we all share

MavDad
October 2016

MavMom (Tracey) worked out so that I could get onto Facebook around this time. I write under Maverick's page as "MavDad." She tied me into multiple grieving-parent groups. I find a great amount of healing in the interactions. I have also found some nuggets that helped me along.

We struggled around Thanksgiving. Every year I would write a Christmas letter to friends and family. What would I write this year? We would include family and children's photos with the letter. What pictures would we include this year? I decided to just be straight with people and wrote the letter. The first part is here:

Christmas 2016

Dear Family and Friends.

This has been a very surreal year for us.

The year was split into two parts. If I wrote this during the first week of June, then I would have included some of the same things that I have over the last ten years. Maverick was doing well in school, driving everywhere, continuing his very social ways and working out four or five times a week. Logan was doing well at Pima Community College, still dabbling in music (taught himself Saxophone and drums), and still working at Walmart. Brenda was still working at PetSmart and thinking about going back to college. Tracey continued focusing on her personal fitness program, leading her monthly book club, weekly volunteering at a bookstore and church, working on her gemologist certification, and keeping the house functioning. She lost her Yorkie (Ziggy) to a hawk or Owl in mid-May which was a struggle for all of us. Fortuitous circumstances brought her in contact with a year old Cockapoo that needed a home. "Ruffles" quickly became a house favorite because of his energy and constant desire to play. I continued with my job at Raytheon. Traveled with Tracey to Hawaii (Kauai) in early

January for work. But we were able to take some time to play tourist.

The second half of the year was very different. Our reality turned to the surreal the night of Friday, June 17, when Tracey and I came home from date night to find Maverick dead. The next two weeks was a blur of shock-based activities: reading over and over his compassionate and heartwarming notes left to be readily found at the time of his death, memorials, helping his friends, gathering all his text and email trails, gathering videos and pictures, and trying to understand while staring into the deep abyss of the hole created in our lives.

In December, we went to Kauai for a third time in fifteen months for my work. We left the house in Logan's hands. It was the first time we left Logan and wouldn't be texting Maverick to make sure he was up for school. We took long walks during my down time looking for heart-shaped rocks (Tracey's new obsession at the time), building rock column memorials in out-of-the-way coves, spreading ashes and leaving wristbands. We had a lot of time to talk about Maverick and our lives. We came home a week later and climbed on a plane with Logan to Colorado. We spent Christmas with Rod and Nancy at their new home in Nebraska and drove to Loveland to spend time with Dottie and Luella. Our first Christmas without Maverick.

An empty chair at the table.

Merry Christmas, Maverick.

We miss our son.

CHAPTER 5

DEFINING OUR "NEW NORMAL"

AFTER CHRISTMAS, TRACEY AND I started a summary phase. We were very active with Facebook groups, grieving groups, awareness groups, and sharing. Tracey more so than I. Those that were farther ahead in their journeys talked about the "new normal." We started defining the concept for ourselves through our summaries.

We felt we probably knew about all we would know about Maverick and the twisted events that led to his death. Although Tracey still reads a lot about the topics surrounding teen suicide and daily devotionals, it only adds slight changes to our perceptions. Having most of the information, we fell into a funk brought on by the continued realization that we can't do anything about this. We can't change this. There isn't anyone to blame. Hitting the "he really isn't coming back" wall multiple times and having mini-Maverick meltdowns. We are left with a huge sense of loss and emptiness. I concluded on one of our evening walks, "Baby, we can keep talking about this all you want. But right now, I just miss him."

Our Maverick meltdowns came with less frequency and were shorter but were the same intensity. We solidified our opinions and beliefs surrounding "What happened to Maverick?" "grief/mourning" in general and "grieving parents" in particular and "society and suicide." Though things change slightly or refine from time to time, we had enough data and information to effectively present a case regarding our opinions. Tracey and I may look at things from a little different perspective, but the fundamental and underlying themes are the same. We regularly receive reaffirmation of our beliefs through our interactions and reading.

What Happened to Maverick?

After reviewing his text trails, interviews with his friends, timeline of events, consulting with experts and checking our perceptions with others, we focus on some basic themes. We know that we will never have all of the story but have centered on these perceptions based on the facts we uncovered.

1) Brain chemistry. Maverick stopped his five- to six-days-a-week strenuous workouts four weeks before his death. He stopped his workout-based diet. His endorphin and serotonin levels were low. He used a steroid nebulizer for a case of bronchitis. The drug used (corticosteroid-based) can cause depression and anxiety. He was able to procure and started smoking marijuana in what appears to be in large quantities. He had also easily obtained high-potency marijuana. Smoking marijuana wasn't something that he did and wasn't a part of his social circle. The impacts to brain chemistry and resulting thoughts, perceptions, and behaviors from marijuana use are well documented. It prevented him from having the confidence and drive to restart his workouts. Marijuana paranoia blocked him from truly exposing his feelings and concerns. Overall, his mental firewall was stripped, which created the "black dot that grew rapidly" that he described in his suicide note to us.

2) School ended and his close friends went on vacation. His social connections slowed down. Although they picked up the last ten days of his life, they weren't as readily available to him when he was first struggling. Not their fault. Several of them (mostly Ben, Zoe, and Tori, some Andrew), upon reestablishing contact with him, regularly texted him about what was wrong. He always had a seemingly reasonable response.

3) Maverick always had a very social connection to the world.
The connection reinforced his self-image and fueled his
confidence. He was saddened by the loss of Ziggy and
Tracey's response to the event. There was a person in his life
that joked and laughed about Ziggy's death. In addition,
this same person would critique and minimize the impact
of Maverick's workouts. Jealousy at its ugliest. We wouldn't
call this bullying as it doesn't appear the person was aware
of the impact of his statements. Maverick's friends said,
"Maverick gave as good as he got." Maverick left a poem
on his phone for us to find the night he died that describes
his feelings.

> There was a sickness in my mind
> Put in by someone too close
> This person wasn't too kind
> And this is why I'll decompose
> He thought of me as this
> And for some reason I believed him
> So I floated into the abyss
> And I became extremely grim
> I wish I could've gotten it out
> But once it was said it stuck
> So I was filled with doubt
> And my life went amuck
> He never felt bad for what he said
> And I think that hurt me the most
> It was lingering in my head
> So I guess here's my ghost
> I tried so hard to ignore it
> But I was reminded every day
> I am truly sorry that I quit
> But I am happy that I'm finally away

4) Girlfriend breakup and female relationship confusion.
Maverick had been dating the same girl for about six

months. Unhappy with the direction of the relationship, he broke it off. However, he kept in contact with her. The text communication shows she knew of his growing depression. They discussed it. She had influence over him and repeatedly told him how disappointed she was that he was smoking pot. He responded with his shame. He was worried he was becoming a "pothead." In addition, one of his closer friends started dating an ex-girlfriend. The way he dropped it on Maverick with "It's okay, right?" disturbed Maverick. He explained his frustration to Logan. Later we concluded that Maverick thought his friend broke the "bro code." He was questioning the long-term viability of a once-close relationship.

5) Fear. Maverick was reluctant to come to any of us about his issues as he was afraid the marijuana use would be found out. He rightfully suspected that we would react harshly. Tracey would play president and try to negotiate. Once she had enough talk, she would send the marines (me) in for a display of verbal "shock and awe." Ultimately, we would find out who gave it/sold it to him and take action. He also wrongfully suspected that we would be disappointed in him if he told us he was depressed.

6) One of the bright spots in Maverick's life the last three weeks was his job hunt. We promised him a car if he got a job. He and Tracey were already looking around. He had his head and heart set on working at Tilly's, a stylish clothing store that targets young adults. He frequented the store and purchased a lot of clothing there. He got an interview, had references (one was Sean, Zoe's dad), and came home excited. They said they would call him back in two weeks for another interview. The two-week date was two days before he died. No call. He was crushed even though we told him that these things take time, give it a week, and we were sure they would call. They called four days after he died. It prompted Tracey to have an immediate mega Maverick meltdown that lingered for a few days.

7) He planned, researched, and we believe he even rehearsed. The facts found that night and his notes appear to support our belief. He identified movies clips and music he wanted played at his funeral. That was left on his phone along with his notes to everyone.

8) He made his decision at least five days before and started writing his notes. He seemed "back to normal" after he made his decision, which is typical of planned suicides. Hence, his normal behavior at my birthday just three days before he died. He left this on his phone, which prompted us into looking closer at time stamps.

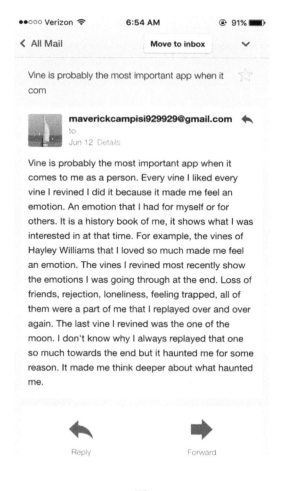

Our conclusion is that Maverick's brain chemistry alteration, combined with social issues, eroding self-esteem, and growing fear of being discovered put him in a corner. We realize there are a million other ways to interpret the information and we have many, many unanswered questions. We struggled with the concept that he may always have had something lurking in his brain and fought many civil wars before losing this one. Did he self-medicate with the marijuana because of depression, or did the marijuana cause it or did it just make it worse? His previous behavior doesn't support previous depression, but we can't be sure. If true, then we are certain that the chemical changes in his brain stripped him of any natural weapons to fight such a war. We circle around the topic now and again, but usually come back to our base interpretation.

Like all grieving parents, we took each new discovery hard. We played the "what if" game for hours. "What if he never got the marijuana?" "What if we found out about the pot or the growing depression?" "What if he couldn't open the locked gun case?" "What if we didn't go to dinner?" "What if he didn't find the ammo?" "What if he had been battling depression all along?" We also played all the "why" question for hours. "Why didn't he tell the truth?" "Why didn't he tell Ben or Logan?" "Why did he even listen to the criticisms of others and not the affirmations from us?" "Why didn't he ignore the comments as was his normal mode?" and so on. All part of the normal "would've, should've, could've" circle that grieving parents run around. Add in a dash of "Was I a bad parent?" and you can see the churning that went on in our thoughts. We still go back to it at times. Usually with tears, confusion, and sometimes anger.

Grief and Grieving Parents

Tracey and I are *not* experts about grief. We have educated ourselves. We actively engage with others that are grieving and mourning. We are particularly active with grieving parents. Through our research and interactions, we have identified common themes that have helped us understand ourselves, our relationship, and our own cycles of grief.

1) Grief, grieving, and mourning is very individualistic. There are common themes. Tracey and I both have different approaches. We recognize and accept that in each other.

2) Grieving and mourning is not in set, linear, time-based phases. Many times we saw people set fixed time frames for their mourning, only to be disappointed. Others would think they are past some predefined "phase" only to find they had circled back and concluded they were stuck.

3) Grieving parents are a special subset of grievers. Parents grieving over the loss of a child to suicide are an even smaller subset with particular characteristics. Most resource information identifies grieving parents as having "complicated grief."

We started identifying "layers." An augmentation of "My Backpack," layers are the things we noticed that influence how individuals grieve based on the elements found in their lives and particular situation. Basically coloring their grief in a way we needed to try to understand if we were to have any empathy past "they lost a child they loved." We started understanding the commonalities and differences. We made verbal lists that I later wrote down, posted, and shared. We received a lot of feedback. We continually refine elements of the list based on our interactions. It has helped us engage with others.

Layers

Age of child
Gender of child
How long ago
Number of siblings
Gender of siblings
Sibling relationships
Birth order of the child
Type of death
First try or other efforts
Location of death

Who discovered child
Warning given (or not)
Last conversation
Last physical contact
Notes left, to whom (good and/or bad)
Parents' marital status/stability
Parents' gender
Parents' perception of child's social status
Parents' perception of child's personality
Parents' support infrastructure
Extended family relationships
Nationality identification
Religious identification
Middle school, high school, college, or not in school
Age/maturity of child (Age <14? 14<Age<19, Age>19)
History of child (school, grades, friends, sports, drug use)
Child's general interests
Child's electronic activities and interests
Child romantically active (or not)
Parent-child connection (Mom, Dad, both?)
Number of pictures/videos/mementos

We use the layer approach as a decision tree when we are speaking with grieving/mourning parents. Parents new to our groups tend to bounce around a lot. Expected as they are still trying to sort their thoughts and feelings into their "story." More about that in a moment.

We started talking more and about the definition of "grieving parents" and looking for common themes. We were actually defining ourselves and our place in society and then checking with others through our sharing outlets. Somewhat to our surprise, we found a lot of common characteristics and approaches.

Every grieving/mourning parent has "My Story." "My Story" is a basic script of what happened before, during, and since the event. Our stories all had elements of all the different phases of grief and mourning you find in literature. The story changes in tone and emphasis based on the phase of the person. We combined the theories and broke them apart while taking in the stories of others. Tracey formulated an overlapping phasing that tied some of the theories together and worked for us: robot, grieving, mourning, and adjusting to the "new normal."

A) Robot. Brought on by shock, this is when the parent is operating to a set mental script as if by habit. Feelings are so mixed and pervasive that they overcome the person such that basic accomplishment of activity requires partial turn off. Usually found in the first weeks and months, or when the person is under stress later. I realized I was in this mode the first two weeks to get through the two memorials and then only at particularly pressing times later. I haven't gone into robot since January 2017. Tracey still falls into this phase occasionally.

B) Grieving. This is the immediate psychological shock. This is the phase that society most recognizes and expects. This is when tears come without prompting. Basic human functions, like eating and sleeping, are a chore or problem. Concentration is muddy. The world is without color, food has little flavor, the person is partially paralyzed mentally. I felt this slightly during my robot phase but really felt it when I came back from Colorado.

C) Mourning. This is a very complicated phase that can take years, if not forever, for a parent. Education materials identify this as the time the person continually adjusts mentally, emotionally, and socially to the change in their life. The parent is adapting. Beliefs, values, and overall cares change. Adjustments come in large waves at first and are quite paralyzing. Decisions need to be made and lives need to be led, yet the brain is clouded with emotions. I bounced back and forth between grieving and mourning until about Maverick's seventeenth birthday. I spend 80 percent to 90 percent in mourning since around the time I wrote "Where Are You, My Son?" which represents a summary of my grief.

D) Adjusting to the "new normal." This is what I define as an acceptance phase. Certain things become a reality. Maverick is not coming back. I won't have any new pictures of him and can only hear his voice and see his antics in videos. The shopping cart won't be full. I don't need to find room for five gallons of milk anymore. I sometimes feel my/our current state is totally unacceptable and bounce back into grieving and/or mourning for short periods.

We use the phrase "grieving parent" as a general label for all parents who have lost a child no matter what phase the person appears to present.

Parents were all asking the same questions and making the same comments surrounding the loss of their child. Tracey and I spent hours in the first three months asking the same questions of ourselves as individuals and as a parenting couple. We found a lot of commonality within many grieving parent groups. The questions seemed to gravitate toward understanding, but also finding and assigning blame. This can be a real danger if the parenting couple starts blaming each other.

A) "Am I to blame?" All parents feel they are the last line of defense for their child. Their minds run along the lines of "my child is no longer here, therefore I failed as a parent." Unfortunately, they believe they have far more awareness and control than we truly master. No matter how seemingly minor, a grieving parent will sometimes latch on to a comment or action that happened prior to their child's death and redefine it out of context. They will then bash themselves for not seeing it and taking action on it. Tracey and I analyzed Maverick's behavior and discussions with us over and over. "When he said/did this, did he really mean that?"

B) "I SWC done ..." Grieving parents will talk in terms of "should've, would've, could've" (SWC). Usually comes right after a particular blame assessment. The thought pro-

WALKS IN THE DARK

cess becomes a bottomless pit because, as Tracey put it to me, "How should, would, could have you taken action on something you didn't even know?" My response, "Aw hell baby, I don't know. I just wish …"

C) "I wish …" and "what if …" This is SWC in a pretty wrapper. I have seen all grieving parents do this from time to time. "I wish …" is a restructure of events believing the outcome would have been different. Maybe for that moment. Maybe forever. Who knows? "What if …" follows the same sort of logic. Tracey and I covered this ground multiple times. "What if he got that job?" "What if we dragged him to dinner with us that night?" "What if he didn't find the ammo?" "What if we bought him a car?" We'd like to think everything would be fine. Our Maverick back, our family back, and our lives back.

D) "My child is perfect." Usually stated by early grievers. We did that as well. We then changed to "Maverick isn't perfect, but he is perfect for us." We found we would discuss his little imperfections when we talked about things we missed. His inappropriate language, his TV on too loud, conning one of us into doing a chore (his laundry), texting Tracey from the other room to bring him food, and his lawyer-like argument style were the things we missed the most. I miss watching him argue with Tracey. Logan and I both signaling him, from behind her, to *shut up* before he got in real trouble or got all "us boys" thrown into the dog house.

Fathers tend to grieve their children from the head and heart. Mothers tend to grieve from their heart and soul. This is a fundamental difference. I yielded to Tracey's grief from the start. She bore him, raised him, and had the most contact with him of all of us. Hence, she still spends time with the above questions and concerns. Like we have seen in Maverick's friends and Logan, she frequently points at herself. This is where the partner has to truly be a partner and not just an observer, or worse yet, a competitive mourner.

Another area of general commonality is our approach to society as well as our perspective of society's approach to us. Very much an "us and them" mentality. I started talking about "non-grievers" like Harry Potter would speak about "Muggles." At first, parents get a lot of attention and then it starts falling off. Non-grievers get on with their lives. The parent is still mourning and wants to talk about their child, what happened, how they're feeling, and their grieving/mourning process. Parents then start seeing friends and family distance themselves or disappear altogether. They feel their child and situation are getting ignored. Grieving parents hear they are wallowing and are told in no uncertain terms to stop talking about it and/or to get over it. People purposely avoid them after they find out what happened.

Especially true for parents grieving a death by suicide. Part of the social stigma. I had one father tell me, "People treat me like I have the plague, am in need of their pity or am some sort of curiosity … like a car wreck." Which brings us to some things that should be said to a grieving parent with great care.

1) "I understand …" or "I know how you feel.…" Unless you lost a child, and especially one to suicide, then you probably don't have a clue. Comparisons to loss of a favorite pet, family member, and/or friend, although sad, are not even close. We, grieving parents, hope you never do understand. The cost of understanding is way, way, way too high. Empathy and compassion are welcome.

2) "He/she is in a better place." And/or "He/she is with God now." The statement may be true and the compassion is appreciated. Nevertheless, a grieving parent feels the best place for their child is at home, at the family table eating dinner and laughing it up with everyone.

3) "When are you going to get over it?" Well, never.

4) "It was his/her time." Ugh. Maybe. So got any ideas how to cope with the loss of twenty-five thousand tomorrows?

5) "Time heals all wounds. You'll be fine soon." Usually comes from a truly empathetic individual saying things will get better. They don't realize a grieving parent has a different

concept of time and a very different concept of the term "heal." For example, grieving parents tend to mark time like the parent of a newborn: days, weeks, months, and years. Started at the day the child died. No matter the time, a grieving parent will tell you it is really "yesterday" for them.

6) "At least you have other children." Thanks. I guess I need to just see my glass is half full instead of destroyed. Which one of your children would you pick to lose?

7) "It could have been worse." This is a true statement. I have talked with other grieving parents that have had it a lot worse. No notes. Impulsive suicide after a minor fight with the parent. Child laid in a coma for days and months. Other people hurt by the child. The list goes on. Nevertheless, coming from a non-griever with the best of intentions, the line is a modified and patronizing form of "Look on the bright side."

8) "Committed suicide." "Committed" is a legal term going back to laws prohibiting "murder of self" usually brought into societies by religious influences. Suicide is generally a person's attempt to end pain. Frequently, the pain of depression. The person, especially a teenager, is not in a mental state that any of us can comprehend. So grieving parents find this phrasing very offensive.

9) Past tense. Things asked or said in past tense ("was") are uncomfortable for a grieving parent, especially if the death is recent.

Grieving parents aggressively defend their child's memory. Many times they will devote more energy to that instead of defending their own emotional state. Mothers much more than fathers. If you think a mom will get aggressive protecting her child, then multiply that by a thousand times to equal a grieving mom protecting her child's memory. Some things that we noticed grieving parents, especially moms, like to experience.

1) Their child's name. This is at the top of the list for a reason. Non-grievers tend to avoid the child's name. One person told me they were trying to be respectful and not hurt me. The reverse is actually true. Saying Maverick's name is an acknowledgment, respectful, and will always get my attention.

2) Saying, "I don't understand, but will listen." This is an opening line for a grieving parent to share. Say it only if you mean it because you will get something in return.

3) Special memories. Grieving parents enjoy sharing special memories or particular aspects about their child.

4) Pictures and videos. A grieving parent will readily share these if asked. Remember anything given by a grieving parent, related to their child, is seen as a gift.

5) Anyone who somehow had contact with the child will get special attention. If there is a special or funny story connected, then all the better.

6) Asking, "How are you doing?" The answer may be terse or open. Either way, you will get bonus points for asking if sincere. A grieving parent can read verbal and nonverbal cues far, far faster than the average population. They will see through you if you are just asking to ask.

A final area of commonality is remembrances. Memorials and mementos are a cornerstone for most grieving parents. They are as varied and individualized as the parent and the child. Significant things, activities, and areas take on a greater significance. A last note written by the child, a favorite pair of shoes, lit candles, grave sites, and the child's favorite food that was purchased long ago are all examples. All the items and physical spaces broadcast "In memory of ..." to a grieving parent. Like the other parents, Tracey and I have a few. Some may call them strange, but we really don't care.

1) "The room." The storage room where Maverick died is a special spot for me. It was the last place I saw him and interacted with his physical presence. It is also the location of my

most life-altering trauma. The blown up pictures from his Arizona memorial are stationed around the room. I put fresh flowers there weekly and visit twice daily to light incense.

2) "The Hat." Maverick had a special hat worn in a lot of pictures. It is an expensive, special style hat that he and Tracey purchased together. We thought we had given it away to one of his friends and panicked. Found out Logan had removed it and several others. He has it in a protected spot in his closet. We have other key clothes he wore and we had picked out special with him.

3) "The tree." I decorated the tree in our entry way the exact way he wanted it his last Christmas with us. It lights up every night. During my grief/mourning transition I felt that if he saw it, then he would know he is home.

4) Peanut butter, body wash, toothpaste, hairbrush, phone, handwritten notes, Taco Bell receipts tucked in my car, and other personal items. Things he last used are still in our home and protected.

5) Tattoos, wristbands, lapel pins, jewelry, and dream catchers. Tracey has over ten tattoos. Tracey and I wear wristbands with his name and dates 24-7 as do many of his friends. I wear an angel lapel pin when I leave the house. We have little dream catchers everywhere. Tracey even has a dream catcher tattoo and had a beautiful dream catcher blanket made for Zoe.

6) Balloons. We have taken to launching helium-filled balloons with attached notes and mini-LED lights almost every Friday night.

7) Public memorials. A tree with plaque in a local memorial park, a bench at his high school, adopt-a-highway (right in front of his high school), yearbook page in his honor, and a scholarship are all examples of public memorials.

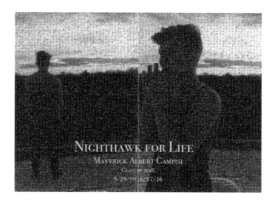

8) Ashes. We have spread Maverick's ashes at locations he visited (Estes Park, high school), where we wanted to take him (Kauai), and where we thought he would be impressed (fountain in front of the Bellagio, Las Vegas).

We love hearing about the things other parents do for anniversaries, birthdays, and special events. Things that others think aren't normal are totally acceptable to us and sometimes copied.

Society and Suicide

Tracey got bit by the suicide awareness bug within two months of losing Maverick. Like any other mom in mourning, she is passionate about Maverick being remembered. A very empathetic individual (Maverick was exactly the same), Tracey also started bonding with other moms. They share wristbands, we took another's ashes to Kauai to spread, she painted rocks with the names of other children and she meets with other moms to discuss topics. She went through a phase when she was consuming statistics and analyzing societies approach (and ignorance) toward suicide. She became especially versed in the area of teen suicide. Our walks and talks were "educating Mike" sessions. She cited the statistics and beliefs with a passion that couldn't be ignored.

Tracey encouraged me to research information myself. I am a "facts and data" guy. The amount of information on the internet is phenomenal. I dug through Center for Disease Control, American Association of Suicidology and National Center for Health Statistics websites among many others. I read articles by experts and government agencies. I crossed-checked my information with Tracey. I summarized my main conclusions.

1) Suicide is the cause of death for 19.3 out of every 100,000 teens. Almost 5,000 teens from 12–19 die from suicide annually; 81% of all teen suicide deaths are male. Females have more unsuccessful attempts.

2) A recent survey of high school students indicates 20% have "seriously considered suicide" with 13% reported creating a plan. Given the average high school contains about 5,000 students, then 1,000 have considered suicide. Scary.

3) Depending on the source statistics, suicide is either the second or third leading cause of death for teenagers in America. A close second to automobile accidents, followed by homicide, and greater than most childhood diseases combined. It actually may be higher. There is such a social and religious stigma around depression and suicide that reported "accidental overdose" and "single car accident" may actually be a hidden suicide. We have interacted with some parents that are too embarrassed to even discuss cause of death. If this was a physical disease, then I believe resources would be pouring in from the public and private sectors, and the press would have it on the front page.

4) Our society has not prepared parents adequately. Parents are well versed with physical sicknesses and injuries. Depression, or mental illness, isn't usually discussed. Manifestations and symptoms are known and sometimes written off as "teenage angst" or "mood swings." The other concern I found on the websites is that the medications intended to help with depression, list depression and suicidal thoughts as a side effect.

5) Our society has not prepared educators properly and puts a lot of responsibility on them. School counselors man-

age out of norm behavior, physical abuse, drug abuse, and bullying. If it brought to their attention. This is a big "if." School counselors and administrators can't see into every child's mind, via behavior, during a standard school day. They need the help of the student body in general.

6) The child/young person's first line of defense is friends. Two blockers here. First, telling an adult is equal to "ratting out" a friend. Second, the friends have even less education than parents and educators. Calling a help line is equal to admitting weakness. We were happy to see that some school districts have awareness programs. Usually set up in response to a community push usually because of a rash of suicides and/or attempts.

7) First responders are ill-equipped to deal with the trauma. These are good caring, compassionate and helpful people to be sure. However, their role is to walk into a "crime scene" and start processing while the family is usually in total meltdown. I can't say enough about the professionalism and empathy of the police officers, detectives, medical examiner, and "compassion professionals" that came to our house that night. But, none of them could really answer the question, "What do I need to do next?" They left some pamphlets and brochures that were somewhat helpful. But, I felt on my own. Luckily, I work for a great company with extensive employee assistance programs. In two phone calls I had answers and definitive direction. In addition, I have a close work friend that had been through this before. What about the other parents that don't have this kind of support? I think every community should have a list of cleared grieving parents that the new griever can contact for guidance and to make sense of all the pamphlets, choices, and next steps.

8) Society has a bias that a suicide means something was fundamentally wrong with the family or the child. Either hidden parental abuse of some sort, bullying, drug abuse, underlying mental illness, or other "out of normal" situa-

tion. Sometimes, but rarely from our experiences and exposure to others, this is the case. Which makes the situation sad on multiple levels. Combined with "it can't happen in my home" mentality in most homes, and you readily see how suicide can happen in any home, any demographic, and any location without the parent even aware that something was wrong. Grieving parents fight this bias all the time. I had these same biases right up to the moment I found Maverick. The realization almost crushed me.

It is easy as a mourning parent to point out all the wrongs. There are solutions. The first and foremost is education. I have told every worried non-grieving parent of a teen the websites (like WebMD) to find information about symptoms. Grieving parents in some of our groups have stepped up calling the press and pressing their school districts to educate and inform the teens; 95% of teens won't call a help line but would readily text a help line. Just texting "go" to 741741 will put them in touch with someone within two minutes. Yet few parents that I know have even heard of such a thing much less talked to their teen about it. Like AIDS in the late seventies and early eighties things need to change from fear to understanding to addressing. Then, like now, the only real way is education.

Tracey is still very active in suicide awareness advocacy. I am very proud of her and gladly give my assistance. For example, she started the MaV movement. She gives out Maverick wristbands that say "Make a Vow. Just ask. Just tell. Text 741741. Call 1-800-273-TALK." I hope that anyone who reads this book will at least look up the symptoms to watch for and how to reach out in their local community. Lives of our young people depend on it.

We realized after Christmas that we were starting to tentatively accept our life situation, our "new normal." Days that we are in a funk. Nights we can't sleep. Constantly feeling like we went on vacation and might have left the stove on. We are very honest about the fact that we don't like our new circumstances. We found some satisfaction and relief interacting and helping others that are going through similar adjustments in their lives. We were pulling our definitions together. We were building a body of knowledge. Sorting things out.

Our new normal: Missing Maverick will never stop. The pain will never end. It won't get "better." It will get "different" and hopefully easier for us to manage.

We just miss our son.

CHAPTER 6

LIVING THE NEW NORMAL

TRACEY AND I STARTED LIVING the "new normal" the period between Christmas and the first anniversary of Maverick's death. There were a few hard times that sent us back into full mourning mode. The first was Tracey's birthday. This year it fell on Friday, February 17, the eighth month anniversary of Maverick and the exact day of the week. What usually is a joyful time in our house turned into a hard day with both of walking about with heavy backpacks. Then came Mother's Day and the day after which was the anniversary we lost Ziggy. Tracey started having numb days with hard days scattered in between.

Most grieving parents will tell you it is the time building up to a significant day that is usually harder than the day itself. At the end of the school year we started feeling the tension build. Our detailed research indicated that was the time, a year ago, when Maverick started having problems. Memorial Day came around which marked a day he had a significant depression-related conversation with his ex-girlfriend that wasn't exposed to us. My birthday, Zoe's birthday, Maverick's anniversary, and Father's Day were coming fast. Each day leading up to my birthday held hard memories for us.

During the time between Tracey's birthday and Maverick's eighteenth birthday, I was finding outlets for my mourning. First, I collected all my little notes about music with intention to compile into a list of songs and their meanings to me. I wanted to put the list into our box of very special Maverick things for others to look at years later. Second, I started making videos, with music, of Maverick's pictures and videos. I would spend hours pulling one together. The music, pictures, and video timing had to be in perfect synch. I guess that is the engineer in me. I would post the videos to Facebook and shared with friends. Many have said, "I didn't know 'Maverick' until I saw your posting. Thank you." Finally, I started writing poems. Mostly for me to explain my feelings over the last year. Spurred on by Tracey and others, I started sharing and posting these as well. In fact, it is the poems that drove people to tell me to write a book.

Music has always been a part of me. I went to high school in Tucson during the 1970s and Arizona State University in the early eighties. It was a time when music was combining and expanding. I played guitar as a youth and music was always on in my house while growing up. I leaned toward rock, country rock, and blues rock. Logan and I have that in common, although he is a far superior musician.

Music has also always been a part of my relationship with Tracey. One of my first gifts to her while we were dating was a cassette of my favorite songs. I would write the words to songs and give them to her. On our twenty-fourth wedding anniversary, nine months before Maverick died, I wrote the words to "Right Here" by Staind and gave them to her. To me, the song represents elements of our relationship. Being a poet, Tracey understands my connection to music. Maverick was starting to influence my taste in music in the two years before he died. I started listening to what is called "Adult Alternative Rock" which is a softer version of modern day "New Wave."

Music and songs move me, heal me, protect me, and represent me. After Maverick died, I became pretty obsessive about music. I discovered love songs, with slight word twists or change of interpretation, represented how I was feeling. Not writing much material as of yet, music was my outlet. I would use the words and sounds, and the emotions they represent, to explain my feelings or how I thought others felt. I would post the lyrics to Facebook.

I drive Tracey crazy with my obsession sometimes. I hear a song and listen to it over and over in an attempt to understand why it moves me or it simply recreates a feeling I had at some point after Maverick died. I absolutely insist she listen to my "new song." She consistently shows her love for me by patiently and politely listening. Sometimes a song will come on the radio in our home while we are eating and we will both suddenly be in tears.

I have an iPod full of these songs. Some are on the Logan defined "slap down" list. Songs that emotionally slap you down to the ground. Guy talk for "this song will make you cry." Here is a list of the top fifteen of over a hundred songs and what they mean to me. The curious can easily obtain them from iTunes.

1) "Forever" by Vertical Horizon. This is a song that came to me two or three days after Maverick died while on a walk in the dark. It is a love song, but to us it represents our enduring feelings about Maverick. We played it at his first memorial.

2) "How to Save a Life" by The Fray. When I first heard this song, I completely lost it. It is an accurate representation of my last talk with Maverick three hours before he died and my resulting feelings shortly after finding him.

3) "Stars" by Grace Potter and the Nocturnals. A soft song about the death of a loved one. Grace Potter delivers an amazingly passionate and emotional vocal. I see pictures of Maverick and I in happy and laughing conversations when I hear the song.

4) "Fix it" by Ryan Adams and The Cardinals. A blues rock song about break up. The chorus reminds me of what I felt the week after Maverick died. I couldn't fix it for Tracey and Logan and it tore me up emotionally.

5) "Heavydirtysoul" by Twenty One Pilots, "Adam's Song" by Blink-182, "Nutshell" by Alice in Chains, "A Strange Day" by The Cure, and "My December" by Linkin Park. These are all songs about suicide, depression, and confusion prior to a suicide attempt. I listened to these songs during the period I was trying to "get inside Maverick's head." I still periodically attempt to answer the question "What was going on in your head, son?"

6) "Get Out" by Frightened Rabbit. This is a song that represents our obsession with Maverick. No matter what we do, he won't get out of our hearts.

7) "Coming of Age" by Foster the People. A song that I perceive Maverick singing/saying to Zoe the last time he saw her. The night before he died.

8) "Suburban War" by Arcade Fire. A song that I perceive Ben would say to Maverick. A song about the loss of youthful friends.

9) "Last Goodbye" by Jeff Buckley. This song takes me to the moment I last said goodbye to Maverick before calling 911. Made the mistake of listening to it before giving a big presentation at work. Ugh. Dumb move. Took me five minutes to collect myself.

10) "Talk" by Coldplay. After I called 911, I needed to talk to someone to reassure me. So I immediately called my younger brother David. Couldn't reach him at first and started to panic. This music and song represents how I felt in that moment. I hear the opening line and usually tear up.

11) "First" by Cold War Kids. A song that Maverick really liked and shared with us. It became a family favorite.

12) "Sweater Weather" by The Neighborhood. Tracey, Maverick, and Ben liked this song. I didn't know about it until after and Tracey shared with me. It is very typical of the type of dance based music Maverick enjoyed. I see him spontaneously breaking into a dance as was the norm for him in our house.

13) "Weight of Love" by The Black Keys. Great love song and great blues based music. It makes me think of Maverick in terms of the rocks in my backpack.

14) "Your Decision" by Alice in Chains. A soft rock song that appears to be about the loss of someone to suicide. I sometimes get angry-sad at Maverick. I see myself telling Maverick the words to this song.

15) "Gone Away" by The Offspring. A song written about the loss of the singer's girlfriend in a car accident. To me it represents what is going on in Logan's heart at times.

The list goes on. I sometimes sing these songs to myself during my walks. I have also found that they will come on in my head when it is too quiet or I am thinking about Maverick a lot. I am very grateful to these artists. They have unknowingly been my counselors.

I started making videos around the time of Tracey's birthday. Started simple, but then became more complex as I mastered the software. Went back through all our electronic pictures, scanned-in photographs, pulled all his videos from family and friends, and started compiling tributes to Maverick, Tracey, and my family. They took a lot of time. I had to have the right picture, right video, right music, and right layout. Tracey showed me how to post them to Facebook. Later, I posted to YouTube (figured that out myself) under the tags "Maverick" and "Maverick Campisi."

After Mother's Day, I started writing poems. I hadn't written a poem since "Where Are You, My Son?" I reached a particularly productive time leading up to Maverick's eighteenth birthday. We were past the one-year mark. I was spending a lot of time reflecting on the past year. Most of the inspiration came from things I felt in summary refined through talks with Tracey and my morning walks. I structured many as open notes to Maverick. I am not a poet. Tracey is the poet. So I bounced ideas off of her looking for a verbal thumbs up or thumbs down. Some were good and some not so good as measured by the responses and feedback from her and others. Here are the ones in unmodified posted form that I would put in the "good" column, with short explanations. Note that on most on-line forums we are known as "MavDad" and "MavMom."

1) "My Crowd." This is a nod to the people in cyberspace that have helped me as I have helped them.

My Crowd

This is my crowd
A cyberspace group
Of broken hearts and confused heads
People that know me
Though we have never met
Because of events we can't flee

This is my crowd
They know what it's like
Smiling all day
While slogging through emotional mud
Exclaiming, "Oh, I'm okay"
Instead of what we really want to say

Our children were all perfect
Yet they had their flaws
The imperfections that made them whole
The things we miss the most
Yet still, perfect souls

We help each other with the pain
The loss of presence
The loss of promise
The everlasting longing
The overwhelming feeling
That we did something wrong

We face society together
Against biases that some of us once held
Fighting for the memory of our children
Showing others that their end
Was no crime or sin

This is my crowd
People I like and respect
Understanding each other's singular wish
Helping work through the Why
Could've, Should've, Would've,
And "If I only tried...."
Shoring each other up
Counting tears we've cried

A salute to my crowd
I wish they were not here
Because I know the cost
But, I am happy they are
For without their insight,
I could truly be lost

MavDad
4/2017

2) "All I Have Left." This is a summary poem. I was lamenting at the time that all I had left of Maverick was a story that started with "I once had a son ..."

All I Have Left
(A letter to Maverick)

All I have left of you
Is a cross with your ashes
That hangs around my neck
Wrist bands that glow
With your name and dates
A life that is sometimes
Caught in an emotional undertow

All I have left
Is the urn on the mantle

Your final remains
Lockets, necklaces, thumbprints
And key chains
All made with care
Given to others whose loss we share

All I have left
Screaming thoughts of my last moments with you
The feeling of stunned helplessness
Thinking "I gotta fix this"
Working so hard to put back
All the damage witnessed
Frustrated realizing I can only say "goodbye"
Not till after I stroked your hair asking you, "Why?"
Blocking your mother's view
From the horror
Of her love, work and plans,
A dream undone
Holding her back while saying,
"We have lost our son"

All I have left
Is the tears of your Momma
In the quiet dark of the night
The panic and sighs of others
When they find out
Of my many thoughts
About the result of your hidden self-doubt

All I have left
Are people that don't say your name, look at us
Or come by
In their fright
That they will say or do something
That will make us cry
Or prompt us to tell them all the why

All I have left
Is your mother, sister, brother,
Friends and family members
That knew you
People I care for
Like we did you
How like us
They miss you too

All I have left
Are pictures of you
And my memories that bring them alive
The wild and crazy videos too
That remind me the sound of your voice
Fighting off confused feelings that you had
Many a different choice

All I have left
Is the room where you crossed
A decorated tree out front
Your stuff and clothes in a box
The hat in your brother's room
Visits from your friends
And your phone
Pleading prayers that you are not alone

All I have left
Is the grief of others
That I feel to my core
And the wonder why you wouldn't know
When you were the one
That always gave people that little bit more

All I have left
Is the memory of our last hug
Your hair the color of the sun

You humming and dancing in the wind
You laughing during our last talk
About things you obviously pushed aside
Because of the sadness you hid inside
Promises of future and words of encouragement
Sadly realizing the last talk was really your good-bye

All I have left
Is knowing that there will be no more
Shaking off daydreams of you walking in the door
You talking me into doing your chore
Precious nuggets and snippets of time
Of all our lives entwined
You maturing into a man
I knew you could be
Things I guess you couldn't see

All I have left
Are my prayers for your peace
Memory segments of time
When all was fine
You were here
And having fun
Growing steady
And swimming in the sun
Your future becoming clearer each day
Life could never take this away
Or steal this happiness from me
Now daily I search for wisdom and grace
Things I struggle to see

All I have left of you
Are our little personal treasures
Mixed with sorrow and sadness
And a hope that is true

Of a time far from now,
I really don't know when,
We will ultimately meet again

Love, Dad

MavDad 4/30/2017
In Memory of Maverick
9/29/99–6/17/16

3) "I Sometimes Dream." I have dreamed about Maverick since a week after he died. Usually three times a month. I share my dreams with Tracey. She has only dreamed about him three times. His lack of dream visitation disturbs her and for a time that was a key topic of our walks and talks. This poem was the result.

I Sometimes Dream
(A note to Maverick)

I sometimes dream
About you in the night
Always happy times
Nothing that gives me fright

We are in a restaurant
You are telling me about life things
What went wrong
And what went right
You always say, "I don't have long"

Or you are showing me
Around heaven
Things you insist I see
Places where people play

Places where people dance
And watch sunsets
A place that you want to stay

I sometimes dream
That you want to come home
We leave the outside lights on
All night
We decorated a tree like Christmas
The whole neighborhood
Sees it glow
So you know where to go

I see you outside the door
You knock and I let you in with,
"Hi, how did you get here?"
You say, "Long story, Dad,
Where's Mom?"
I point to our room
You blow by me and head that way
Always saying, "I have to leave real soon"

You are sometimes in passing cars
I turn around to catch up
You keep going fast
But you give me a wave
And a smile
Something for me to save

Your Mom doesn't see you
In her dreams
And it bothers her
Why don't you come to her?
Do you think it will cause a scare
Or cause her to scream?

I always told you,
"She is far, far stronger than she seems"

You need to visit her
In her dreams
Tell her you are okay
Tell her nothing is wrong
Tell her you miss her
And see when she cries
And you still care
And you watch over her
When she is not aware

I sometime dream about you
It is all I have left
Is my brain just processing
Or am I going crazy
Either way, I enjoy our conversations
Your smiles that still brighten
Your visits lighten my emotional load
Especially when you say,
"Stay the course, Dad,
You are on the right road"

MavDad
7/9/17

4) "A Picture." The beginning portion actually happened. I
went into a daydream. Just sitting in our living room and
something pushed me to look under the chair.

A Picture

I found an old picture
Stuck under the chair

I closed my eyes for a moment
And I was suddenly there

You were rounding third
On the triple you hit
Coaching third I told you to stop
You blew right by me
And scored the run
Coming back to me you said,
"Did you see that? It was fun."

I flashed to a later time
You and I playing ball
You blocked my shot
"Foul!" was my call
You just strutted saying,
"Oh! Maverick the defender.
That had to hurt."

I streamed to a million moments later
You telling a story at the table
Of course you had to swear
Mom said, "Maverick! Language!"
But, you didn't care
You winked at me with a "watch this"
And went on a tear
Your brother and I laughing so hard
Until your Mom gave us all "The Glare"

My mind clicked to us
Walking in the desert
Hunting rattlesnakes
Me worried about you getting bit
And having to tell your mom
You babbling on and on
About girls, music, mysteries of love

And all that is cool
Oblivious to my worry
Protecting Mom's jewel

I jumped to us playing darts
On that rainy afternoon
The first time you beat me
Me in Arizona State maroon
You in "the hat" and bare foot
Doing your little dance
When you tallied the score
Giving me the "got you that time" smile
As you headed for the door

We were suddenly driving
To teach you to parallel park
I hear the music
I say it is getting dark
You say you got this kicked
You learned playing Grand Theft Auto
It gave you every skill you need
Me shaking my head and saying,
"Oh, please, God, help me"

I look at the picture
Just a nugget of gold
As every picture is
For me it is new even though it is old
I found it under the chair
And I don't know why I looked
Was it you, God or just something in the air
That told me something is there
A gift because how I told Mom I miss you
Just yesterday
Or my feelings that all start with "sad"

Moments when I was simply
"Maverick's Dad"

I'll file the picture in my memory
I have a little book
Times I can make come alive
It, like your Mom, are the things
That help me survive and thrive

MavDad
7/21/2017

5) "My Broken Heart." An explanation of my grieving/
mourning process. This poem came from a comment made
by someone at work that I spoke about with Tracey. We
talked about it for a while that night. I composed it over
two days during my walks.

My Broken Heart

I have been trying to fix my broken heart
Been working on it for a while now
I have some experience:
A friend going south when I went north
My mother gone when I needed her
A close cousin dying in a war
A beloved dog gone to a snake
I was able to make repairs
Take out a little "heart glue"
Put the pieces back together
No experience prepared me for this

I remember the moment it broke
Watching in slow motion
As a crystal glass fell to the floor
Shattered to a million pieces

My mind beginning to blur
Watching your Mom's face change
When her glass hit the floor
Over days and months gathering pieces
Shards, fragments and chunks
Hers and mine

There are so many pieces
Some can only be seen with a microscope
This one is him in my backpack for twelve hours at
    Disney
This one is excitement and smiles
When he caught his first fish
That one his first home run
That one his first perfect parallel park
And that one is his smile
Sigh, his first solo drive
MavMom and him playfully arguing
He's gonna lose
I can't figure out where they all go
Put one on only to take it off
Try another

I sometimes don't have all the right tools
Have to ask MavMom for help,
She holds the pieces while I try to glue
Listen to music,
Try to remember the times clearer
Listen to others that share the same task
They know about other tools
Or looking for shooting stars as answers
From him or God

I get frustrated and break off a piece
It doesn't look right.
Start again.

Sometimes I learn about something new
The fragments change shape. Sigh
Sometimes I am working on it so hard
Nothing else matters

I sometimes help MavMom with hers
Tools I found
Shards I know that fit
Things we have in common
Things that she describes
Same frustrations
"Put it down for now, baby,
We can work it later"

Others try to help by telling me about their
Broken heart and fixes
Loss of a dog, Aunt or parent
Those are things I know how to fix
They mean well
They just don't understand

I may never put my heart back together
I wonder if I fear completion
Or will miss looking at the individual pieces
I feel that the end result
Will have a lot of gaps and holes
Reserved for things he would fill in the future
An unfinished heart

For now I will continue working
For there is so much left to do
So many pieces to glue
I know others are doing the same
And I will try to help
I'm not the quitting type
So, "Put it down" won't happen.

Maybe one day I will mend my
Broken heart
Just won't be today.

MavDad 8/2017

6) "Under the Surface." A poem summarizing the things
going on in my head at different times. I tied together my
experiences, and my many thoughts about them, refined
during my walks and separate talks with Tracey.

Under the Surface

Under the surface
Of my very presence
Is a swirl of activity
A culmination of all the trials
Of the last fourteen months

It started the moment
I found my son
Everything changed
Never before more confused,
More angry
More sorry
More empty
And yet in control
Putting aside what I saw
Though it dug at my soul
Like an eagle's claw

Taking care of all that night
Planning all social expected events
Over the next several weeks
Dealing with others
That looked at me with fright

Listening to my wife cry at night
Remembering my focus
That he must be honored
Have to keep it together, keep it tight

Spending months asking questions
Of my son and his life
Answers I knew
And some a surprise
Listening to my wife
And her insight
Trying to pull together
A comprehensive answer
To "Why did he end his life?"

I crawled into his world
His last three weeks
Through reading, and writing
His friends and music
Looking for why he changed
What drove him
Why didn't I see
As I knew him
And he knew me

I kept going with my life
My responsibilities to others
Sometimes ignoring the pain and void
Sometimes not having a choice
Loss on the surface

And the tears flowed
And I sang to him on my walks
And I yelled at him in the night

And I begged God for answers
Some I have, some I never will
"Thy will be done" sometimes
Seems very unfair

Here I am
14 months gone by
I won't ever be the man I use to be
In some ways better
And some ways worse
Unyielding in my faith
My vows
My commitments
And mission to help others
Anything else would not honor him

I will continue
To channel the swirl
That moves under my skin
Into something useful
So that God will judge me worthy
To see him again

MavDad August 2017

7) "Things I Said." I was doing a lot of reflecting the weeks leading up to Maverick's eighteenth birthday. Tracey and I were talking a lot about our last year. Different things I said at different points in time were continuously replaying in my head. This came to me right after I finished one of my walks. Standing on the drive, I was staring at the lit up tree outside his room with Coldplay's "Fix You" playing in my head. Composed as a note to Maverick.

Things I Said
(A note to Maverick)

Some things I said
Play in my mind
From the start
Always trying to be kind
Output of a heavy heart

Things I know you heard
An angry dad
Or a sad dad
Trying to figure things out
Mostly said to your mom
Just blurting things out
Attempting to help
Not to do harm

"Oh, God, no. It's Maverick."
Said when I found you
Blocking your mom
Like I thought you wanted
Standing tough to her wrath
Calculating the aftermath

"We have lost our son"
Said to your mom
While holding her back
Listening to her sobs
And screams in the night
I know the sound filled you with fright

"I can't fix this, Maverick. Why?"
The last thing I said to you
As the police came up the drive
Introducing you to the officer

As if you were still alive
Walking away thinking
"No stroke, heart attack or shock,
Must remain calm,
Have to take care of Mom"

"He is yours but also mine,
Tell me he is in heaven and fine"
Said to God on my early morning walk
Just two days later
Immediately seeing a shooting star
The answer that made me whole
Yet I daily pray for you
Happiness and peace for your soul

"Our Maverick, our child, our loss,
But your rules,"
Said to your mom
Outside the funeral home
She was worried about cost
And honor
And memories
And not making a mistake
You heard me assure her
"We will work it together
For his namesake"

"Where did I go wrong?
This can't be real!
I have lost my son!"
I shouted outside
To your brother and Mom
My first Major Maverick Meltdown
They are quite rare
Now I feel them coming
And know to take care

And to think it through
You see them calm me
When angry at and about you

"We all have backpacks
With "Maverick" stenciled"
Babbling about rocks and balloons
To your mom, sis, and bro
My explanation of grief
Result of you leaving too soon

"I didn't get a vote"
I said to your grandpa
With tears in my eyes
He said, "I know"
With tears in his

"You made a huge mistake, my son.
But I will always remember
Your smile
And am sad you alone
Walked your last mile"
Said on a dark walk
Another shooting star
Felt you weren't far

"He wasn't perfect,
But he was perfect for us"
Didn't want you idolized
It is your imperfections
Humorous inappropriateness
Expensive style
That made Mom and I
Always walk that extra mile

"My heart is broken
See, I carry it around in a bag"
Said to a friend
That tried to understand
I know that brought a smile
To your face

"Fine. But not in a way
That you will never know"
Said to a group
They try to engage with me
As you know
They just can't see
The inside of me.

"I pray to God you never do"
When someone says,
"I just don't understand"
At least they try
Bonus points for that
Nothing said by them
Can made me cry

"Men miss their children
From the heart. Women miss their
Children from the soul. So
I will protect 'MavMom' till my time to go"
Explaining to an executive
That asked about my loyalty
To your mom

"What the heck is this?"
When I found the Christmas light
While cleaning my car
Something done at least
A dozen times

How did it get there?
No matter
Thanks for the sign
I carry it and feel better

There are many other things
I know I've said
I know you have heard them all
Phrases and moments
That jump into my head
Your Mom reminds me
Makes sense of my babble
And listens to my new "favorite song"
And tells me "We can do this"
Although the days seem very long
Without you to follow along

MavDad
Sept 2017

8) "I Asked God." The week before Maverick's eighteenth, I was struggling. Caught in a vacuum of perpetual sadness over the loss of all I thought Maverick was to become. I was talking to God, Jesus, saints, and angels a lot. I reflected back on my talks with God since Maverick died and this popped into my head.

I Asked God

I have always talked to God.
He answers in his own way.
Expecting me to interpret
Through an open heart
Signs, words of others, and song
When I can't focus
Helping me along

I have asked a lot
Since our son passed
Our Maverick
Like a die was cast
He always answers
And reminds me of my task

"Why did you take my son?
My wife's ray of sunshine?"
God said, "I didn't take your son.
I prepared you and your house.
You need to see and understand
Maverick was always mine,
From start through all time."

"Why didn't you stop this?"
God said, "Oh, I tried. Roadblocks
And cautions. Like all, he has free will.
Try as I may, he didn't see the toll.
He meant no harm to you
As you know,
Just think it through."

"Where did I go wrong?"
God said, "Your mistake is that you
Thought you had control
Of his heart and soul.
Your Maverick wasn't 'Maverick'
At that point.
As you now very well know."

"Why didn't he see we love him?"
God said, "He knew and knows.
I know you loved and love him.
I know you cared and care for him.
I see your pain and the sorrow

In your home.
I lost a son too
I know the cost
And am sorry for your loss."

"Do you hear me? My family hurts.
We need your care."
God said, "Do you hear me?
Why can't you just be still?
I have always been here.
I have always cared
And all here see your hidden tears
And the tears of your wife
And hear the screams of your souls
I am always in your life
Always here.
Listen with your heart
And my messages and signs
Will all be clear."

"What do I do from here?"
God said, "Stay the course
And take care of all you hold dear.
Listen to me and don't resist.
And answer my call
When others need an assist
I won't let you falter or fall
As your journey is not done.
I will watch over and guide you all.
While you grieve for your son
And what he was to become."

MavDad
Sept. 2017

9) "I Remember." Written for Maverick's eighteenth birthday. Eighteenth birthdays are significant events in our house. It is the point when Tracey and I firmly put our children on the path to adulthood. We start talking about colleges in earnest. Maverick's eighteenth had extra significance for us as he is the youngest. We would be preparing to be empty nesters. As a father, I lamented the loss of so much promise and skills that I knew would be significantly stronger by this point in time. Friday, September 29, was one of the saddest days I experienced in months. I am including the note I posted with the poem.

Today is Maverick's eighteenth birthday. During my last conversation with Maverick, three hours before he died, we discussed what I thought he would be at eighteen and how important this day would be. He smiled politely and summarized with, "That sounds very cool, Dad." He has been gone 469 days.

Thanks to MavMom for letting me bounce ideas off her ... especially since the discussions were very hard for her on multiple levels.

Happy birthday, Maverick.

I Remember

Eighteen years old
And I still remember
All your history as if foretold

Born a warm Az day in September
Mom and you struggled
And gave me a scare
Suddenly there and bundled
Neither of you worse for wear

Our ten trips to Disney World
Are thoughts I like to share
You asleep in my backpack
Brother sleeping in my arms
Walking back after fireworks
My legs screaming alarms

You asleep on me
Outside Downtown Disney Cirque Du Solei
You and your brother mastering a coup
Allowed only one purchase a day
But would somehow end up with two

Playing baseball with you
In my heart a special place
Practicing for hours then
Mom in the dugout
Me on third base
Watching you hit doubles and triples
Smiling as you gave chase
To scoring and the all-stars
Always forgetting to tie your lace

You quitting because basketball
Became yours and then ours
Answering the daily call
To play one-on-one and shoot baskets
Until I could barely crawl

Moving back to AZ
Having a hard time finding a house
And the right school
You insisting on a pool
Choices limited and costs were high
But you had to have it "to stay cool"

Shaking my head with a deep sigh
"Oh, and it has to be heated too"

You grew up so fast
High school already
Helping you pick each class
Our last in line
On the final path of youth
Worried about grades, friends and girls
Your social skills we have proof
Our house's beloved goof
Moments made of gold
Times of constant laughter
In our little stronghold.

Teaching you to drive
In my new car bought by mom
You picked it up quickly
I worried you were too sure of yourself
You passing first time so slickly
Big smile on your face
Mom and I with cheers and tears
Our baby growing at a rapid pace

Hunting rattlesnakes, playing darts,
And martial arts
You pushing your friends in grocery carts
Inappropriate language and jokes,
Friends over every night
You growing through stylish clothes so fast
That my credit card shook with fright
Lifting weights, playing video games
Running with your crowd
Coaching us on all your friend's names

All this and more I would tell you
One on one, as I anoint you a man
On this, your day of days
And tell you, "If you truly try, then you can"
Things remembered and words of wisdom
Things I see so clear
Meant to help you persevere
Definitions of respect, honor and integrity
And taking care of your family
And staying true
To the ones that love you
Never turn from family or friend
That is facing an attack
And always remember
We have your back
Things told you
Over and over before
Summarized
And put into your core

Things now only your brother
Will know
Words etched by a father
On his son's soul
Saved special for this day
To pull you firmly off youth's path
And start you on your adult way

Then we would throw a party
With all your friends
Give you special gifts
And show you your new used car
Telling you to be mindful
And not to stray too far

Yet I sing "Happy Birthday" alone
Sitting In the room you chose to leave
Crazily hoping you'll call on my phone
Wiping my tears on my sleeve
Staring at your picture
The candle, flowers and incense
Thinking in conjecture
Wondering what went wrong
Choking through singing the song
Saying "Happy 18th Birthday my son
We love you and miss you very much
And the man we knew you'd become."
On this, your day of days
Maverick, I so wish you were home.

MavDad
9/29/2017

You can see how the things I spoke about previously weaved into my poetry. My writing, my manifestation of mourning, is an attempt to articulate the essence of my experiences and feelings.

Grieving/mourning parents like to receive feedback. I receive different feedback from grieving parents and non-grievers. Grieving parents could relate to my song interpretations and felt many of the same emotions. Non-grievers, except for friends and family members that knew Maverick in the last two years, were pretty silent. I must have seemed a little crazy to them. Grieving parents readily share photographs and videos of their lost child. We always respond to each other as silence is considered very rude when a grieving parent shares a photo, memory, and/or specific fact about their child. So my video creations got a lot of responses about Maverick's looks, style, outgoing nature, and enthusiasm. Non-grievers sporadically responded. Always polite and supportive, but with less enthusiasm than "My Crowd."

My writing and poems got more of a universal response. Both groups would comment that a particular piece moved them and/or was a great tribute. Grievers, understandably, were a little more enthusiastic and would thank me for words they needed. Many would repost my composition on their own websites. It was nice to get the feedback and attention and was happy when others found my words helpful. Nevertheless, the person's feedback that means the most to me is Tracey's.

Many have said that Maverick's death unlocked hidden talents. I should be happy about that fact and use it to the fullest. I don't know if it is talent. I am still trying to understand the meaning of "happy."

I still miss my son.

Chapter 7

Moving Forward

MAVERICK HAD A GREAT LIFE. He is our youngest. Blond hair, blue eyes, his own style, quick wit, enthusiasm, and an overabundance of social skill, he never ceased to capture and keep our attention. Like all our children, any child, he had behaviors and characteristics that we attempted to groom and grow while he was growing up. He also had some that we tried to curb. After reviewing his history in the context of our overall family, Tracey and I concluded that we are good parents. We kept track of everyone's activities, pushed them into needed experiences, are still mindful of their likes and dislikes, and never left them guessing about our expectations. We are not perfect parents. We hover, can be opinionated, and are over protective at times. All in all, we loved and cared for all of them the best we know how.

These days, the last two years of Maverick's life are what we tend to focus upon. Who he was during that period is what we miss the most. He was growing and maturing at a rapid rate. His social and physical confidence was very high, his world was expanding rapidly, and he became phenomenally entertaining. He was doing the right things to improve himself and assist in the lives of others. Tracey and Maverick grew very close. Recognizing and applauding this relationship, I started talking with him about how I expected him to emotionally take care of his mom, many years from now, when I am gone. Logan and Maverick became confidants and partners. They spontaneously created comedy routines before our eyes at the dinner

130

table and breaking out in dance when they heard a cool song. He was on the right path. Tracey and I were laying out our plans for the things he would need and want in the coming years.

The night Maverick died was an understandably massive turning point in our lives. Shocking and shattering our lives as well as the lives of family and friends that all knew him. Tracey and I often wonder what would have become of our Maverick if those three weeks never happened. Like all parents I suspect, we believed he would have stayed on the same trajectory. He would have gotten a job and car, kept running with his crowd of friends, kept growing out of expensive clothes and would need more, graduated high school, gone to college, fell in love, got married, and eventually presented us with a group of blond hair, blue-eyed grandchildren. All along he would challenge us with parental trials and tribulations that we feel we always had the skills and means to address. We lament the devastating loss of potential. A piece of our future is gone.

Tracey, Brenda, Logan, and I have been through so much since Maverick's death. Looking at ourselves as individuals and as a family group, working through grief and mourning though our individual channels, losing family and friends and gaining others, facing society and the suicide taboo, maintaining our family bond, supporting each other through Maverick meltdowns, breaking old habits and developing new ones, accepting and attempting to help others. We look at ourselves and realize how we have changed. All the reading, sharing, educating and manifestations of mourning have significantly modified who we are, thought we were, and will be. Some days it is a bit much to think about and fully comprehend.

Tracey and I are Maverick's parents. We love him very much. It is an enduring love. He is still alive in our hearts. We feel it every day. Much of our distress and confusion is that our hearts feel a strong love, but our heads can't understand why he is not here. Since we know we will love him forever, then will have to live with the heart/head disconnect forever. We continue seeking outlets for the conflict. Tracey's new slogan is "Love Lives Forever." Our love for Maverick will live forever.

So this is our story. At least, so far. At the last "Out of the Darkness" suicide awareness walk sponsored by the American Foundation for Suicide Prevention (AFSP), Tracey and I were talking about what grieving/mourning parents call "the journey." We decided to define it as an endless train tunnel. There is always a light at the end of the tunnel. Sometimes dimmer, and sometimes bigger and brighter, but always there. The light, for us, is Maverick. We know that for the rest of our lives we will miss our Maverick.

May he rest in peace.

PICTURE LIST

Cover picture taken by Mia Schneider with Maverick on the roof of our house looking at sunset, Aug 2015.

Dedication picture taken by Maverick. You can see him in my glasses. Santa Monica Beach, California.

Chapter 1 pictures in order:

Tracey and Maverick. Maverick is about 3 months old.

Brenda, Logan, Maverick. Maverick's first Halloween. Largo, Florida.

Maverick asleep on Mike outside Cirque Du Soleil, Downtown Disney, Orlando.

Maverick and Pluto. Magic Kingdom, Disney World. Maverick is four.

Maverick at MGM Grand, Disneyworld, Orlando. Sword is his second purchase of the day.

Maverick, age 6. Rehearsal Dinner for Cousin Kristi and Jerry DeFalco. West Palm Beach, Fla

Maverick, age 9. Professional picture. Growing his hair. McKinney, Texas

Maverick, age 9, and Tracey and Mike. First place baseball trophy. McKinney, Texas

Basketball before very first game. Maverick, almost 11. McKinney, Texas

With Tracey on cruise ship. Mav is 6. Miami, Florida

In Jamaica. Coffee Plantation Tour

Miami with Mike and Logan

In Grand Cayman right before Para Sailing

Yukon, Alaska. Mav is 11.

Campisi clan at Estes Park. Taken by Dottie Depperschmidt (Grandma D).

With Logan stomping around Rocky Mountain National Forest.

In the pool he insisted we get with the house in Az. 2012

With Logan at Logan's graduation. Maverick is 14. 2013

Mav at 14, throwing his normal sign. 2013

Mav and Logan at Estes Park. Almost 15. Taken by Tracey. One of my favorites.

With Logan outside Coors plant in Golden, Colorado.

Mav with Top Gun shirt on USS Midway, San Diego. 2014

With Andrew on USS Midway, San Diego. 2014

Cali. With Logan on Hollywood Walk Of Fame. Dec 2014

Cali. With Tracey on Santa Monica Pier, California. Dec 2014

Cali. With Tracey and Mike. Santa Monica Beach, California. Dec 2014

With Ben Smith. Suns vs. Celtics game. Phoenix, Az. Mav is 15. 2015

With Ben at lunch. Ironwood Ridge High School, Oro Valley, Arizona. 2015

With Logan hamming it up. Taken by Tracey. 2015

With Logan laughing at a joke played on Tracey. Taken by Tracey. 2015

At Anytime Fitness working out. Taken by his trainer. 2015

With Tracey in living room before going to work out. 2015

At Big Thompson Dam, Colorado. Summer of his 15th year. 2015

Being teased by Logan. Big Thompson Dam, Colorado. 2015

Video screen shot. Maverick's 16th birthday. Sept. 29, 2015

Hamming it up with Tracey in our kitchen. 2015

Selfie. One hour after getting his driver's license. Nov 2015

Putting gas in my car. Taken by Tracey. Feb 2016

With Zoe at school. Screen shot from "Equals Awesome" video. 2015

Mav "showing" he is tired of Tracey taking selfies. Chilli's, Az. March 2016

Black and white in our back yard. 2016

With Tracey. Selfie by Tracey. 2015

With Ziggy. Mav is 10. Mckinney, Texas

In my car. Mav at 16. 2016
On our roof. 2016
With Ben at movies in Phoenix. Taken by Ben's Grandmother. June 2016
Last picture of Maverick. Taken while he was completing work promised to Logan. June 10, 2016

Chapter 3 pictures in order:

Ruffles laying just inside Maverick's bedroom door
Screen shot. Walking the casket out at end of service.
With Dottie Depperschmidt (Grandma D) at Estes Park, Co. 2014
With Rod Depperschmidt (Grandpa D) in back yard. Loveland, Co. 2015
MAC carved by Maverick in Birch. Front of Grandma D's house. Loveland, Co.

Chapter 4 pictures in order:

Tracey's "Love, Maverick" and awareness tattoo.
Brenda's "Maverick Wave" tattoo.
Gift cup from Tracey to Mike
Tracey's car
Hannah Pastor at first "Out of Darkness" walk.
With Mike at Estes Park. Got tired of Tracey taking pictures.
Maverick looking at sunset from our roof.
Christmas tree with Maverick picture.
Rock monument with wristbands. Kauai, Hawaii.

Chapter 5 pictures in order:

Outside garage storage room.
Maverick's Tree and "The Hat". Tree is decorated like Xmas.
Turtle tattoo representing Maverick. Done in Kauai, Hawaii.
Page in 2017 Ironwood Ridge High School yearbook.

Chapter 7 picture:

On the way to dinner on Saturday night. Tracey selfie with Mav. One of my favorites. 2016.

Back Cover: Maverick on 9/29/2015. His 16th birthday. Tracey took the picture.

About the Author

Michael Campisi is a business executive and an Arizona native that has lived all over the world. He has a bachelor of science degree, masters in business administration, and multiple industry certifications.

He married Tracey (Depperschmidt) Campisi over twenty-six years ago and is the father to their three children: Brenda, Logan, and Maverick. They live in Oro Valley, Arizona, a suburb north of Tucson. Since light pollution ordinances minimize streetlights, Michael takes his daily 4:00 a.m. solitary walks in pure darkness. This appeals to him as he loves to look at the stars, constellations, and the occasional shooting-star. It gives him time to pray, work out his plan for his workday, and think through pressing issues.

After the death of his youngest child and second son, Maverick, Michael's walks are full of thoughts and action options surrounding the struggles, trials, and stresses presented to his family by the loss of so much value and promise. Michael and Tracey are very active with teen suicide awareness, suicide prevention, and other grieving parents.

CPSIA information can be obtained
at www.ICGtesting.com
Printed in the USA
LVHW06s0730240518
578355LV00027B/640/P